Other titles in this series

THE BEST
IN TENT
CAMPING

**A GUIDE FOR CAR CAMPERS WHO HATE RVs,
CONCRETE SLABS, AND LOUD PORTABLE STEREOS**

TEXAS

Wendel Withrow

MENASHA RIDGE PRESS
BIRMINGHAM, ALABAMA

Library of Congress Cataloging-in-Publication Data
Withrow, Wendel.
  The best in tent camping, Texas : a guide for car campers who hate RVs, concrete slabs, and loud
portable stereos / Wendel Withrow.
    p. cm.
  Includes index.
  ISBN-13: 978-0-89732-684-1
  ISBN-10: 0-89732-684-9
    1. Camping—Texas—Guidebooks. 2. Camp sites, facilities, etc.—Texas—Guidebooks. 3. Texas—
Guidebooks. I. Title.
  GV191.42.T4W48 2009
  917.64—dc22

                          2009023994

Cover and text design by Ian Szymkowiak, Palace Press International, Inc.
Cover photo courtesy of © Alamy
Cartography by Steve Jones
Indexing by Ann Cassar

Menasha Ridge Press
P.O. Box 43673
Birmingham, Alabama 35243
www.menasharidge.com

TABLE OF CONTENTS

THE BEST TEXAS CAMPGROUNDS

THE BEST
TEXAS
CAMPGROUNDS
[continued]

ACKNOWLEDGMENTS

Thank you to:

The many dedicated and under-appreciated state and federal employees who shared their favorite campsites with me, so I can pass them on to you. A special note of appreciation to Darcy Bontempo and the technical staff at Texas Parks and Wildlife Department for the excellent detailed maps of the state park campgrounds.

Molly Merkle, Holly Cross, Annie Long, Steve Jones, Scott McGrew, and the whole team at Menasha Ridge for their assistance in tackling a project the size of Texas.

Clarke Abbey and the legendary Edward Abbey (1927–1989) for permission and inspiration to share the most important message of all: "Sentiment without action is the ruin of the soul. One brave deed is worth a thousand books."

Lee Stetson (Yosemite's John Muir), Doug Peacock (*Grizzly Years*), and Jack Loeffler (*Healing the West*) for their tireless efforts to defend America's remaining wild lands and pass on the passion of John Muir, Edward Abbey, and countless unsung conservationists to future generations of tent campers and all who love our natural world.

My legal assistant, Donna Ervin, for her technical expertise in preparing the manuscript and never complaining about the extra work.

My research assistants and traveling companions, Philip Rothermel and Nick Wood.

My parents, Alvin and Lucy Withrow, for passing on to me their love of history and travel along with the confidence to meet any challenge.

My wife, Ada Marie, for her assistance at many of the campgrounds and patience at home where the park files and stacks of background documents seemed to just grow and grow.

ABOUT THE AUTHOR

Wendel Withrow is a native Texan and began treks into the woods at a young age. During his years at the University of Texas at Austin, where he received a B.A. in History with high honors, Wendel began his camping career and a wanderlust that has taken him to the most beautiful parts of Texas. After receiving his law degree from Texas Tech School of Law, he continued to search out the lesser-known natural won-

ders throughout Texas and the United States. In 1989, he stumbled upon *Desert Solitaire* by Edward Abbey and his love for the outdoors was transformed into a crusade to save all things wild while any remained to be saved. Joining the Sierra Club, Wendel used his passion for pho- tography and inspiration from Abbey to rise to chair of the Lone Star chapter of the Sierra Club; he is currently chair of the Dallas group of the Sierra Club. Wendel continues to seek adventure in the outdoors and is currently research- ing the Native American tribes of the desert Southwest and the natural won- ders located in the sovereign nations of North America's first citizens.

Any author who takes on the writing of a camping guidebook for the state of Texas is asking for a serious challenge under the best of circumstances. Add in $4-per-gallon gas and two hurricanes worth of natural destruction and . . . well, you get the picture. Fortunately, I received assistance from all over the state to narrow my search for those special tent-camping areas where RVs were either nonexistent or at least kept at a tolerable distance. As many of you readers know, finding such a place is becoming more of a challenge, but the good news is that our park authorities also treasure these hidden enclaves of solitude and understand the need for tent campers to have their own separate spaces to enjoy nature's curative powers unencumbered by massive mobile homes complete with sewer systems and satellite dishes. However, I was pleased to see a few RVs with solar panels, so maybe there is hope . . . maybe.

In choosing the 50 tent campgrounds included in this guide, the process was not only based on the criteria explained in the Introduction but also on that feeling we all get when we leave the cement jungle for an outdoor adventure and find something special. It may be a spectacular vista, a fiery sunset, a single flower bloom, or even the intoxicating smell of a campfire, but we all sense it as soon as we arrive. As you visit the places described in this simple book, I can only hope you will have the same sense of wonder and receive the gifts of peace only the natural world can instill.

You will also see a listing of diverse books (some hard to find) and selected quotes from various authors who have come before us and contemplated the eternal struggle between the seemingly unquenchable appetite of modern civilization and the very real need of the individual to leave that world and return to a simpler life, even if just for a short time. This section is entitled Voices from the Campfire and relates to one of the most important traditions of tent camping—*conversation!* Whether it's between childhood friends or new acquaintances, gathering around a crackling wood fire and sharing life's experiences without a computer screen or cell phone to separate us from our fellow humans is the best type of escape. To assist in that escape is the essence of tent camping and the purpose of this book.

—*Wendel Withrow*

Whether you are a new arrival or a native Texan, it doesn't take long to recognize the size and diversity of the Lone Star State. From the High Plains of the Panhandle to the tropics of South Texas, the state stretches an amazing 906 miles from north to south. From the desert climate of El Paso to the towering piney woods of East Texas, a mere 841 miles will connect you. While this guidebook covers a lot of those miles, it is impossible to know every perfect tent campground, and I'm quite sure some were missed. In fact, there are probably many sites known only to the few who have had the good fortune to find them but wisely don't invite the entire state to join them in their special place of solitude. I understand and respect that. We all need that one secret place to escape to.

The good news is that Texas is so big that we can all find our own haven in the hills or valleys. Whether you love the deepest woods, the driest desert, the tallest mountain, or the unlimited seashore, this book will help you find a place to claim as your own.

THE OVERVIEW MAP AND OVERVIEW-MAP KEY

Use the overview map on the inside front cover to assess the exact location of each campground. The campground's number appears not only on the overview map but also on the map key facing the overview map, in the table of contents, and on the profile's first page.

The book is organized by region, as indicated in the table of contents. A map legend that details the symbols found on the campground layout maps appears on the inside back cover.

CAMPGROUND-LAYOUT MAPS

Each profile contains a detailed campground layout map that provides an overhead look at campground sites, internal roads, facilities, and other key items. Each park entrance's GPS coordinates are included with each profile.

GPS CAMPGROUND-ENTRANCE COORDINATES

Readers can easily access all campgrounds in this book by using the directions given and the overview map, which shows at least one major road leading into the area. But for those who enjoy using the latest GPS technology to navigate, the necessary data has been provided. To collect accurate map data, each park entrance was recorded with a handheld GPS unit. Data collected was then downloaded and plotted onto a digital USGS topo map. Each profile includes the GPS coordinates in two formats: latitude/longitude and UTM. Latitude/longitude coordinates tell you where you are by locating a point west (longitude) of the 0° meridian line that passes through Greenwich, England, and north or south (latitude) of the 0° line that belts the Earth, the Equator.

The UTM coordinates index a specific point using a grid method. The survey datum used to arrive at the coordinates is WGS84. For readers who own a GPS unit, whether handheld or onboard a vehicle, the Universal Transverse Mercator (UTM) coordinates provided with each campground description may be entered into the GPS unit. Just make sure your GPS unit is set to navigate using the UTM system in conjunction with WGS84 datum.

UTM COORDINATES: ZONE, EASTING, AND NORTHING

Within the UTM coordinates box in each campground description, there are three numbers labeled zone, easting, and northing. Here is an example from the Abilene State Park profile:

> UTM Zone (WGS84)   14S
> Easting   417199
> Northing   3567466

The UTM zone number (14) refers to one of the 60 vertical zones of a map using the UTM projection. Each zone is 6° wide. The zone letter (S) refers to one of the 20 horizontal zones that span from 80° South to 84° North. The easting number (417199) indicates in meters how far east the point is from the zero value, which runs north-south through Greenwich, England. Increasing easting coordinates on a topo map or on your GPS screen indicate you are moving east; decreasing easting coordinates indicate you are moving west. Since lines of longitude converge at the poles, they are not parallel as lines of latitude are. In the Northern Hemisphere, the northing number (3567466) indicates in meters how far you are from the equator. Above the equator, northing coordinates increase by 1,000 meters between each parallel line of latitude (east-west lines). On a topo map or GPS receiver, increasing northing numbers indicate you are traveling north; decreasing northing coordinates indicate you are traveling south.

THE RATING SYSTEM

Each campground description includes a rating system for beauty, site privacy, site spaciousness, quiet, security, and cleanliness, and each attribute is ranked with one to five stars with five being the best. Of course, these are subjective, but I've tried to select campgrounds that offer something for everyone with a general rating system for comparisons only. For instance, two stars is acceptable; three stars is very good; four or five stars were only awarded to premier campgrounds.

BEAUTY   Exceptional scenery can be found throughout Texas, but the five-star campgrounds will provide breathtaking views—you will know you're in a special place. The campground will be situated for full enjoyment of the view, which may be a towering mountain range or the prefect forest pond or stream.

PRIVACY   Ideally, trees, shrubs, and other natural features will be left in place or incorporated into the site development to offer privacy and barriers between adjacent sites. The best campgrounds have well-spaced sites with little visual contact between neighbors and a sense of solitude due to the campground's distance from the nearest roads, towns, or RV section.

SPACIOUSNESS   Spaciousness indicates room for two tents away from the parking area. There should also be space for separate areas to cook, eat, and just relax without being on top of your neighbors.

QUIET   Our top rating for quiet means little or no overhead or road noise, minimal social noise, an aura of solitude, and quiet hours. It was a plus if we could hear the water from a nearby river or stream, birds singing, or the wind through the trees. Quiet is a difficult attribute to quantify since we all know it can change quickly, depending on your neighbor.

SECURITY   Many of the parks have an on-site host or park rangers regularly checking the campgrounds and received higher ratings. The entrance stations were also staffed during daylight hours for increased security.

CLEANLINESS   Everyone wants to see clean restrooms, fire pits, and picnic tables and a campground free of ground litter. If the tent site was well maintained and the restrooms and showers of more recent construction, the campground received higher marks.

FIRST-AID KIT

A useful first-aid kit may contain more items than you might think necessary. These are just the basics. Prepackaged kits in waterproof bags (Atwater Carey and Adventure Medical make them) are available. As a preventive measure, take along sunscreen and insect repellent. Even though quite a few items are listed here, they pack down into a small space:

Ace bandages or Spenco joint wraps

Adhesive bandages, such as Band-Aids

Antibiotic ointment (Neosporin or the generic equivalent)

Antiseptic or disinfectant, such as Betadine or hydrogen peroxide

Aspirin or acetaminophen

Benadryl or the generic equivalent, diphenhydramine (in case of allergic reactions)

Butterfly-closure bandages

Comb and tweezers (for removing ticks from your skin)

Emergency poncho

Epinephrine in a prefilled syringe (for people known to have severe allergic reactions to such things as bee stings)

Gauze (one roll)

Gauze compress pads (six 4- x 4-inch pads)

LED flashlight or headlamp

Matches or pocket lighter

Moleskin/Spenco "Second Skin"

Pocketknife or multipurpose tool

Waterproof first-aid tape

Whistle (it's more effective in signaling rescuers than your voice)

HELPFUL HINTS

Be sure you are equipped with a state highway map, and if you're venturing off the main roads, a copy of Mapsco's County by County Road Atlas is a must have, along with any state park, forest service, or national park maps available online or at the entrance station. Topographical maps and a GPS system are also highly recommended for any serious hiking.

In many parts of Texas, rain may come at any time, but keep in mind that weather patterns are most likely to change in the late afternoon. High winds may kick up with little warning, so stay alert if you're enjoying a day on the lakes or rivers. Spring or summer afternoons often bring intense rainstorms with lightning followed by spectacular sunsets. Overnight storms can also be a real surprise, so be sure to stake down your tent and put up your rain fly. Know what to do and how to seek safe shelter when these storms hit. In an emergency, use your car for immediate shelter, but be aware of low-water crossings and the danger of flash floods. Tornadoes also require special precautions, so know where to find the closest sturdy structure.

Of course, the weather is part of what makes Texas such a great place to camp, but it also provides its main danger—*heat.* As in many southwestern locations, a large number of Texas's best hiking trails not only provide a significant physical challenge but also the dangers of heat exhaustion and heat stroke. Don't be fooled by cool mornings or a few clouds. Always carry a hat, sunscreen, trail snacks, and more water than you might think. A good rule is two to four quarts per person per day, but even this is a bare minimum where temperatures may approach 100°F by noon. The best advice is to hike very early in the morning or late in the afternoon to avoid the brutal midday sun. Then spend the rest of the day under the trees or in a local spring-fed pond or river. Camping and hiking in Texas, even in summer, can be a highly rewarding experience if you respect the elements. Remember, even the rattlesnakes seek cover in the hot summer sun. You should do the same.

Speaking of rattlesnakes, be extra alert in any outdoor setting in Texas for not only rattlesnakes but also copperheads and a few other snakes such as coral snakes and water moccasins. Your best defense is to watch where you step or reach, and when you do see a snake, or any wild animal, leave it alone. They're just as unhappy to see you, so go around and let them be.

Also, many Texas parks have healthy crops of poison ivy, which may grow along trails and in less-maintained sections of the camping areas. Learn to recognize the three-leaf pattern and steer clear! If you do get into a patch, washing the affected skin with alcohol, soap, and water can prevent the rash from developing. If you know you get the rash easily, always wear long pants when hiking through underbrush and carry an alcohol-based hand sanitizer and a washcloth. Be sure to eventually wash off shoes and anything else that may have the oil on it. If you are exposed to poison ivy, raised lines or blisters will usually appear within 12 hours (but sometimes much later), accompanied by a terrible itch. Refrain from scratching because it can cause infection, but it won't spread the rash, as is commonly believed. Wash and dry the area thoroughly. Various over-the-counter products will alleviate the symptoms until it heals on its own. In worse cases, a doctor can prescribe treatment.

So now that your head is full of facts, pick up the crew, purchase a Texas Parks Pass ($60) or a National Parks and Federal Recreation Lands Annual Pass ($80) for one year of unlimited free entrance fees, and enjoy the best tent camping in the Lone Star State. These passes are available at most entrance stations or visitor centers and provide the best way to enjoy and share the 50 special places described for you and your family.

BIG BEND COUNTRY AND
THE GUADALUPE MOUNTAINS

1
ABILENE STATE PARK

LOCATED **AT THE CROSSROADS** of Texas history, Abilene State Park is surrounded by low limestone hills in a rugged area used first by the Tonkawa and Comanches to hunt buffalo and later by Texas cowboys leading cattle drives on the Goodnight-Loving Trail. On your way to the park, a stop at the restored Buffalo Gap Historic Village takes you back in time to an era when tent camping was not recreation but a requirement for traveling across the vastness of West Texas, including a stop on the legendary Butterfield stage route. This line of early communication ran through the hunting grounds of several Native American tribes who recognized that these latest arrivals were a serious threat to their way of life. The name Buffalo Gap refers to a break in the hills used by migrating buffalo. The local tribesmen's dependence on the buffalo ultimately hastened their downfall as the vast herds of buffalo were replaced by the Texas Longhorn.

As you leave headquarters on the Panhandle Plains Wildlife Trail, the first right turn leads to the swimming pool area and beautiful rock structures built in 1933 by Civilian Conservation Corps Company 1823, consisting of World War I veterans who found themselves unemployed during the Great Depression. In 1935, this company also included black veterans, a CCC first in Texas. Be sure to examine the water tower, pool buildings, and picnic areas to appreciate the workmanship and heavy labor of these former soldiers.

Returning toward the main road, stay right at the fork toward Cedar Grove tent campground on your left. This small campground is hidden in a thick grove of evergreen cedars that not only provides welcome shade, but more importantly, protection from the West Texas wind. While all the sites are good, look for sites 39, 40, and 42 at the back of the circle drive. These sites have a little more space and back up to some

> *Buffalo Gap Historic Village takes you back in time to an era when tent camping was not recreation.*

RATINGS

Beauty: ☆ ☆ ☆
Privacy: ☆ ☆ ☆
Spaciousness: ☆ ☆ ☆
Quiet: ☆ ☆ ☆
Security: ☆ ☆ ☆ ☆
Cleanliness: ☆ ☆ ☆

ADDRESS:	150 Park Road 32 Tuscola, TX 79562
OPERATED BY:	Texas Parks and Wildlife Department
INFORMATION:	(325) 572-3204
RESERVATIONS:	(512) 389-8900; www.tpwd.state .tx.us
OPEN:	All year
SITES:	12 (Cedar Grove); 21 (Pecan Grove)
EACH SITE:	Picnic table, fire ring, lantern hook, central water
ASSIGNMENT:	Reservations get you in the campground, but first come, first served on site choice
REGISTRATION:	At headquarters
FACILITIES:	Swimming pool; modern restrooms
PARKING:	At each site
FEE:	$10 per night at Cedar Grove (water only); $4 entrance fee ages 13 and above
ELEVATION:	1,993 feet
RESTRICTIONS:	*Pets:* On leash only *Fires:* Fire rings only; check on burn bans *Alcohol:* Prohibited *Vehicles:* 2 per site *Other:* Maximum 8 persons per site; guests must leave by 10 p.m.; quiet time 10 p.m.– 6 a.m.; bring your own firewood or charcoal; limited supplies at Buffalo Gap; pick up main supplies in Abilene; gathering firewood prohibited

heavy brush and a dry creek bed. The sites are also within a short walk to the large family-friendly swimming pool.

Returning to the main road, turn right and watch for the numerous armadillos poking around for a snack. Travel 0.8 miles into the heart of the park over low water crossings to Pecan Grove sites 62 through 84. This area has electricity and some RVs, but the massive pecan trees shade most of the sites, which also have large, level tent pads. Look for sites 74, 75, and 79 for the most privacy and easy access to the Elm Creek Nature Trail and the Eagle Trail.

As you leave the park, turn left on FM 89 for access to Lake Abilene, along with a close-up view of massive wind farms generating clean electricity from that always-reliable west Texas wind still carrying the history of westward expansion.

RECOMMENDED READING

Indian Tribes of Texas by Rupert N. Richardson and Dayton Kelley, 1971.

VOICES FROM THE CAMPFIRE

"I hope to God you will not ask me to go to any other country except my own." Barboncito, Navajo Chief, speaking to General Sherman in May 1868—more than four years after the Navajos were removed from their ancestral homes at Canyon de Chelly (Utah) and forced to make "The Long Walk" to Bosque Redondo (New Mexico). Recognizing the failed policy of "relocating" herdsmen to desert farming, a treaty was signed allowing the Navajos to return to the lands within The Four Sacred Mountains where they live and thrive today.

MAP

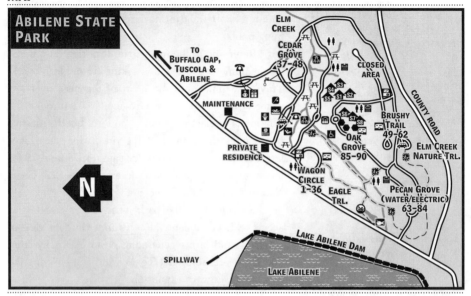

GETTING THERE

From Abilene, drive south on FM 89 to Buffalo Gap. Turn left on Park Road 32 to reach the entrance.

GPS COORDINATES

UTM Zone (WGS84)	14S
Easting	417199
Northing	3567466
Latitude	N 32.2408°
Longitude	W 99.8789°

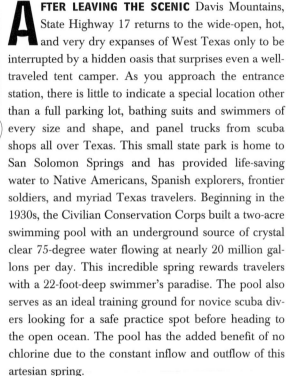

This incredible spring rewards travelers with a 22-foot-deep swimmer's paradise.

AFTER LEAVING THE SCENIC Davis Mountains, State Highway 17 returns to the wide-open, hot, and very dry expanses of West Texas only to be interrupted by a hidden oasis that surprises even a well-traveled tent camper. As you approach the entrance station, there is little to indicate a special location other than a full parking lot, bathing suits and swimmers of every size and shape, and panel trucks from scuba shops all over Texas. This small state park is home to San Solomon Springs and has provided life-saving water to Native Americans, Spanish explorers, frontier soldiers, and myriad Texas travelers. Beginning in the 1930s, the Civilian Conservation Corps built a two-acre swimming pool with an underground source of crystal clear 75-degree water flowing at nearly 20 million gallons per day. This incredible spring rewards travelers with a 22-foot-deep swimmer's paradise. The pool also serves as an ideal training ground for novice scuba divers looking for a safe practice spot before heading to the open ocean. The pool has the added benefit of no chlorine due to the constant inflow and outflow of this artesian spring.

After leaving the pool, the water flows by small canal into a newly restored *cienega,* or desert wetland, that is home to the endangered Pecos Gambusia and Comanche Springs Pupfish. This area, once destroyed, is now being restored by Texas Parks and Wildlife and other partners to its original location and function as a living ecosystem downstream from the pool area. Given its location in a desert, the vegetation is also truly unique, including cattails, rushes, and reeds.

The campground begins just to the left of the pool parking lot and contains RV sites until sites 14 through 19 in the back right corner. These spacious sites hold a number of tents. It's not exactly a wilderness experience, but the miracle of water in the desert will help your body

RATINGS

Beauty: ✪ ✪
Privacy: ✪ ✪
Spaciousness: ✪ ✪ ✪
Quiet: ✪ ✪
Security: ✪ ✪ ✪ ✪
Cleanliness: ✪ ✪ ✪

recover from those mountain hikes in Big Bend, Davis Mountains, or Guadalupe Peak, which surround this little-known but refreshing watering hole. The wide-open views and lack of wind breaks around this campground will require some extra staking, but a visit to this two-acre swimming pool in summer is well worth it. Be sure to bring your lawn chairs, swimming gear, and sun protection so you won't be suffering overnight in your tent. Also, be aware that while the summer days can easily exceed 100°F, nights cool off quickly.

RECOMMENDED READING

The Tree Army, A Pictorial History of the Civilian Conservation Corps., 1933–1942 by Stan Cohen.

VOICES FROM THE CAMPFIRE

"Our task is to widen our circle of compassion to embrace all living beings and all of nature" (Albert Einstein).

KEY INFORMATION

ADDRESS:	P. O. Box 15 Toyahvale, TX 79786
OPERATED BY:	Texas Parks and Wildlife Department
INFORMATION:	(432) 375-2370
RESERVATIONS:	(512) 389-8900; www.tpwd.state.tx.us
OPEN:	All year
SITES:	32
EACH SITE:	Water
ASSIGNMENT:	Reservations get you in the campground, but first come, first served on site choice
REGISTRATION:	At headquarters/entrance station
FACILITIES:	Picnic tables, covered shelters, fire rings, upright charcoal grills
PARKING:	At each site
FEE:	$11 for tent sites; $7 per person entrance fee
ELEVATION:	3,248 feet
RESTRICTIONS:	*Pets:* On leash only *Fires:* Check for burn bans during dry weather *Alcohol:* Prohibited *Vehicles:* 2 per site *Other:* Maximum 8 persons per site; guests must leave by 10 p.m.; quiet time 10 p.m.–6 a.m.; bring own firewood or charcoal; limited supplies at park store; pick up necessities in Toyahvale, Ft. Davis, or Pecos; gathering firewood prohibited

MAP

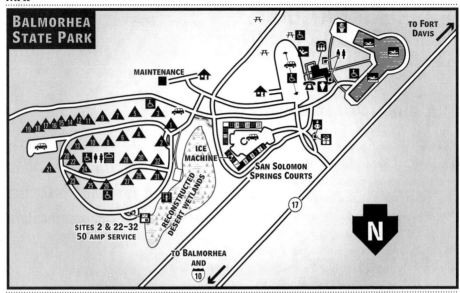

GETTING THERE

From Ft. Davis, travel North on TX 17. From I-10, exit on TX 17. Travel south until you see the park on your left.

GPS COORDINATES

UTM Zone (WGS84)   13R
Easting   617495
Northing   3424122
Latitude   N 30.9447°
Longitude   W 103.7700°

3
BIG BEND NATIONAL PARK: CHISOS BASIN CAMPGROUND

WITH A CAPTIVATING PANORAMIC VIEW of the Chisos Mountains, the Chisos Basin Campground is one of the most popular camping areas in Big Bend National Park. Turning right off the main park road, a winding road leads down past the pay/information station and into the campground. Follow the road by keeping to the left until the "no generator zone" begins around site 48. Although there are a handful of acceptable tent sites in 1 through 47, the best sites are 48 through 60. Site 59 is secluded, with relaxing shade and an excellent view of the surrounding peaks, while site 60 is quite spacious, perfect for a family or small group. Site 55 is hidden from the road and has its own trail to the restroom. If you're here to explore the park, any site will do if you arrive late and don't get your first choice. After choosing your location, feed the pay station and begin your exploration of one of the most remote and scenic national parks.

There are many hiking trails in Big Bend, and some of the best are near the Chisos Basin area. Most notably, Window Trail has one of the trailheads located in the campground itself. With a round trip of 5.6 miles and a moderate uphill return, the trail is well worth the effort to see the postcardworthy Window View. Other trails in the area include the Lost Mine and Basin Loop. Near the other trailhead to the Window Trail and Basin Loop is the visitor center, store, restaurant, and lodge. The visitor center is informative, and the restaurant provides a wonderful breakfast buffet in case of a rare rainstorm or other good excuse not to cook.

Wildlife around the campground is quite diverse. Mammals include the piglike javelina, jackrabbits, skunks, black bears, and even mountain lions. Ask a ranger or read the numerous signs to find out what to do if you encounter a bear or lion. Also, be sure to use the bear box and keep a clean campsite.

> *Limited tent sites and a little noise pollution is a small price to pay for the breathtaking landscape on all sides.*

RATINGS

Beauty: ✿ ✿ ✿ ✿ ✿
Privacy: ✿ ✿
Spaciousness: ✿ ✿
Quiet: ✿ ✿ ✿
Security: ✿ ✿ ✿ ✿
Cleanliness: ✿ ✿ ✿ ✿

KEY INFORMATION

ADDRESS:	Big Bend National Park P. O. Box 129 Big Bend National Park, TX 79834
OPERATED BY:	National Park Service
INFORMATION:	(432) 477-2251
RESERVATIONS:	(877) 444-6777; www.recreation.gov
OPEN:	All year
SITES:	60
EACH SITE:	Picnic tables, bear box/food locker
ASSIGNMENT:	First come, first served
REGISTRATION:	Self-pay station
FACILITIES:	Flush toilets, centrally located drinking water, dishwashing sink, showers at Rio Grande Village Campground only
PARKING:	At campsites and next to restrooms
FEE:	$14 per night; $20 park entrance fee
ELEVATION:	5,401 feet
RESTRICTIONS:	*Pets:* On leash only *Fires:* No ground fires or wood fires allowed *Alcohol:* No public consumption *Vehicles:* Cars, vans, trailers, RVs; tent camping only in "no generator zone" *Other:* Maximum 8 people per site; quiet time: 10 p.m.–6 a.m.; 14-day camping limit; no smoking on trails

Chisos Basin Campground is the most highly visited campground in Big Bend thanks to the rugged mountains and relatively cool temperatures. Therefore, the campsites fill up quickly and the camper seeking to get away from the hustle and bustle of the city may feel a little too close to their neighbor. However, the limited number of tent sites and a little noise pollution is a small price to pay for the breathtaking landscape on all sides.

RECOMMENDED READING

Hiking Big Bend National Park by Laurence Parent.

VOICES FROM THE CAMPFIRE

"In all these travels I intend to walk off the beaten paths, hike off the trails, bushwhacking in body and mind to see the world anew—it was the way I decided to live the rest of my life" (Doug Peacock, *Walking it Off—A Veterans' Chronicle of War and Wilderness,* 2005).

MAP

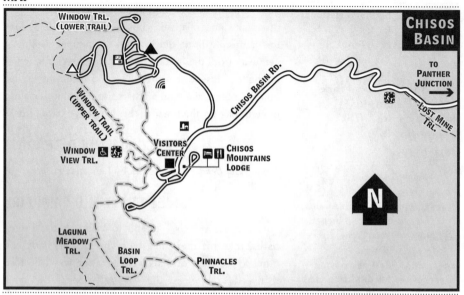

GPS COORDINATES

UTM Zone (WGS84)	13R
Easting	665055
Northing	3239684
Latitude	N 29.2753°
Longitude	W 103.3010°

GETTING THERE

From Marathon, go south on US Highway 385. Proceed past the Persimmon Gap Visitor Center and turn right at Panther Junction. Keep traveling 3 miles until you get to the Chisos Mountains Basin Junction, and turn left. Follow the road 7 miles until you come to the Chisos Basin Campground. Turn right and follow the road to the campground. Stay to the left until you see the "no generator zone" and tent sites 49 through 60.

4
BIG BEND NATIONAL PARK: RIO GRANDE VILLAGE AND COTTONWOOD CAMPGROUNDS

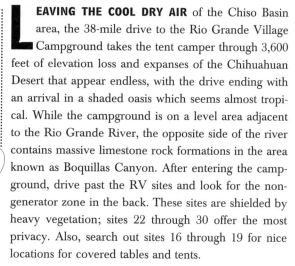

In winter don't miss incredible bird-watching opportunities here with more than 450 confirmed species.

LEAVING THE COOL DRY AIR of the Chiso Basin area, the 38-mile drive to the Rio Grande Village Campground takes the tent camper through 3,600 feet of elevation loss and expanses of the Chihuahuan Desert that appear endless, with the drive ending with an arrival in a shaded oasis which seems almost tropical. While the campground is on a level area adjacent to the Rio Grande River, the opposite side of the river contains massive limestone rock formations in the area known as Boquillas Canyon. After entering the campground, drive past the RV sites and look for the non-generator zone in the back. These sites are shielded by heavy vegetation; sites 22 through 30 offer the most privacy. Also, search out sites 16 through 19 for nice locations for covered tables and tents.

When considering camping at Rio Grande Village, be aware that temperatures and humidity from May to September are probably not pleasant for tent camping, but winter months allow not only for good overnight stays but also for incredible bird-watching opportunities in an area with more than 450 confirmed species. The joy of desert hiking is also greater in the wintertime. If a cold blast does come through, however, be sure to visit the hot springs located 1.9 miles off the park road as you approach the main campground and park store. Another worthwhile side trip is the 4-mile drive to Boquillas Canyon Overlook and the Rio Grande River as it turns almost north to complete the big bend which gives this national park its name. A final note on visiting this area of the park: Remember that the traditional informal crossing of the river to visit and trade with Mexico is now strictly prohibited.

Return on the main park road toward the Chisos Mountains Basin Junction and continue straight to enjoy more wide open spaces in Big Bend National Park. This well-paved but lightly traveled road takes

RATINGS

Beauty: ✿ ✿ ✿ ✿
Privacy: ✿ ✿ ✿
Spaciousness: ✿ ✿ ✿
Quiet: ✿ ✿
Security: ✿ ✿
Cleanliness: ✿ ✿ ✿ ✿

you to some of the most scenic parts of the park. However, if you are looking for primitive campsites, dirt roads to your right will take you to Government Spring, Grapevine Spring, Paint Gap, and Croton Spring campgrounds. Be sure to inquire at the Panther Junction Visitor Center about road conditions or any other helpful information about these remote desert areas.

Back on the main road, turn left at the Castolon/Santa Elena Junction and view the Chisos Mountains towering on your left. Also, take notice of the Sam Nail Ranch and Homer Wilson Ranch and try to imagine the hardships these early settlers faced. Just walk the short trail to the Wilson Ranch for a history lesson in desert survival. Likewise stop at Sotol Vista Overlook and Mule Ears Viewpoint to experience a landscape some may view as a barren expanse, but is one that contains a wide variety of flora whose beauty is only enhanced by the toughness necessary to thrive in this arid region. If you visit in spring and early summer, the display of flowering prickly pear cactus, desert willow, ocotillo, and yucca will have your cameras out to record the surprises in this barren world.

As you pass the Castolon Visitor Center (which is closed in summer) and the park store (open all year), proceed 0.8 miles to the Cottonwood Campground turnoff on your left. This open expanse of a campground does not provide much privacy and the tents are mixed with the RVs and trailers. However, the central area does provide an area of trees and grass for tents. There is also a resident band of javelinas known to assist with camp cleanup should you forget to do so. This campground sits right on the Rio Grande River and is a winter home for bird-watchers from around the world.

As if to make up for the absence of private tent–camping sites, leave the campground and continue 8 miles along the main road toward Santa Elena Canyon, one of the more famous sites in the National Park System of the United States. Take the Santa Elena Canyon Trail across a sandy creek bed and get a great view of the river as it emerges from between sheer 1,500-foot cliffs. This trail is less than 1 mile in length, but hiking

KEY INFORMATION

ADDRESS:	PO Box 129 Big Bend National Park, TX 79834
OPERATED BY:	National Park Service
INFORMATION:	(915) 477-2251
RESERVATIONS:	(915) 477-2291 for non-RV information
OPEN:	All year
SITES:	93
EACH SITE:	Picnic table, upright grill, bear box
ASSIGNMENT:	Reservations get you in the campground; site choice is first come, first served
REGISTRATION:	Self-pay station
FACILITIES:	Flush toilets, drinking water, showers, washer/dryer near park store (open all year)
PARKING:	At each site
FEE:	$14 per night; entrance fee of $10–$20 for a 7-day pass
ELEVATION:	1,830 feet
RESTRICTIONS:	*Pets:* On leash only *Fires:* Charcoal and stoves only; no ground or wood fires *Alcohol:* Prohibited *Vehicles:* 2 per site *Other:* Maximum 8 persons per site; quiet time: 8 p.m.–8 a.m.; bring your own charcoal; limited supplies available at park store; pick up main supplies in Marathon or Ft. Stockton; gathering firewood prohibited; visitor center closed April–November

MAP

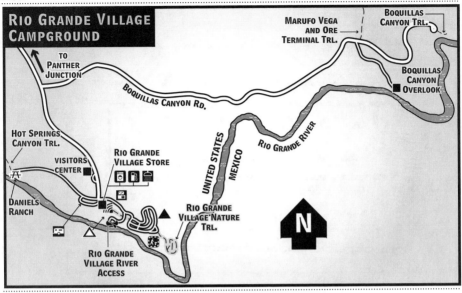

RIO GRANDE VILLAGE CAMPGROUND

MARUFO VEGA AND ORE TERMINAL TRL.

BOQUILLAS CANYON TRL.

TO PANTHER JUNCTION

BOQUILLAS CANYON OVERLOOK

BOQUILLAS CANYON RD.

HOT SPRINGS CANYON TRL.

RIO GRANDE RIVER

RIO GRANDE VILLAGE STORE

VISITORS CENTER

UNITED STATES

MEXICO

DANIELS RANCH

RIO GRANDE VILLAGE NATURE TRL.

N

RIO GRANDE VILLAGE RIVER ACCESS

GETTING THERE

RIO GRANDE VILLAGE CAMPGROUND:

From Marathon, enter the park on US 385, turn left at Panther Junction, and travel 20 miles to Rio Grande Village.

GPS COORDINATES

UTM Zone (WGS84) 13R

Easting   698663

Northing 3229744

Latitude   N 29.1808°

Longitude W 102.9570°'

it is a great way to end a trip to Big Bend or just to whet your appetite for more desert camping under the stars and the shade of towering cacti.

RECOMMENDED READING

The Journey Home—Some Words in Defense of the American West by Edward Abbey, 1977. Chapter 3: Disorder and Sorrow contains the perfect description of back-road travel in Big Bend starting near Castolon and Cotton-wood Campground.

VOICES FROM THE CAMPFIRE

"I made our bed in a dusty clearing in the cactus, but my beloved refused to sleep with me, preferring, she said, to curl up in the back seat of her car. The omens multiplied and all were dark. I slept alone under the shooting stars of Texas, dreaming of rocks and shovels" (Edward Abbey).

MAP

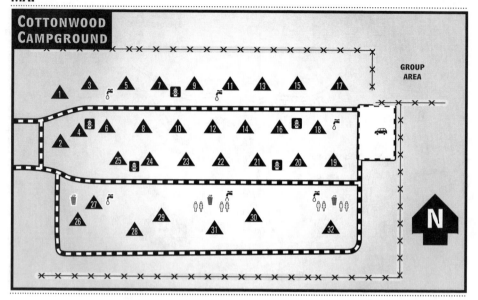

GETTING THERE

COTTONWOOD CAMPGROUND (CASTALON):

From Lajitas or Marathon, travel to Castolon/Santa Elena Junction inside Big Bend National Park. Drive south for 22 miles on the Ross Maxwell Scenic Drive. The campground is 0.8 miles past the Castolon Visitor Center.

> *Be on the lookout for wild animals, such as deer and javelinas, that live in this wonderfully remote park.*

LOCATED IN THE SHADOW of its better-known neighbor, Big Bend Ranch State Park is an idyllic escape for those seeking a tent camping site along the scenic Rio Grande River with easy access to FM 170. Whether you're coming from Presidio to the Northwest or Lajitas and Big Bend National Park to the Southeast, the rugged beauty of this seldom-traveled road as it cuts through Colorado Canyon makes up for any lack of fancy campground amenities along the river. This road makes numerous low water crossings. Keep on the lookout for loose livestock, rockslides, and wild animals such as deer and javelinas, that live in this wonderfully remote park. It's also home to eagles, falcons, and migrating birds that come for the mild winters along the river. If you're looking for even more solitude and a true desert experience, bring your four-wheel-drive or other high-clearance vehicle and travel to the interior of the 300,000 acres on Casa Piedra Road, F.M. 169. This 30-mile stretch of roadway will lead you to 12 primitive sites with hiking, mountain biking, and equestrian trails. There are showers near the historic lodge and Bunk House at Sauceda, but be sure to check in with the park to make sure they're accessible to primitive campers. The campsites have no water or electricity, so bring all needed supplies. You'll be rewarded with a wilderness experience and solitude usually reserved for backpackers.

Returning to FM 170, scan the rocky hillsides for herds of desert mountain goats traveling these steep heights with incredible ease. The main tent campgrounds are located at Colorado Canyon, Madera Canyon, and Grassy Banks. These sites also offer river access for the large number of rafters and canoe groups that wait patiently for the water level to rise. However, always call ahead if you're counting on a river trip—this desert river is unpredictable, but worth the wait.

RATINGS

Beauty: ✿ ✿ ✿ ✿
Privacy: ✿ ✿ ✿
Spaciousness: ✿ ✿ ✿ ✿
Quiet: ✿ ✿ ✿
Security: ✿ ✿
Cleanliness: ✿ ✿ ✿

As you travel along FM 170, the lush greenery along the banks is in stark contrast to the rugged cliffs towering above. All three campgrounds are adjacent to the river and benefit from the only shade within miles. The sandy soil also makes for a soft tent floor, and there is a compost toilet at each location. If you are looking for serious day hiking or a place to camp prior to backpacking, Colorado Canyon provides the best access to over 25 miles of true wilderness on the Rancherias Trail. There is also a river trail between Colorado Canyon and the other two tent campgrounds, Madera Canyon and Grassy Banks. These last two also allow trailers, but the lack of electricity and sewer hookups keep most RVs away.

Whatever your interest, this relatively new park will provide even the most rugged outdoor enthusiast in your group a significant physical challenge and solitary experience.

RECOMMENDED READING

The Big Bend of the Rio Grande by Ross A. Maxwell, 2008.

VOICES FROM THE CAMPFIRE

"The Spanish explorers were lured by tales of cities whose streets were paved with gold, and their imaginations were fired to such an extent that they were willing to endure almost unbelievable hardships to realize their dreams" (Ross A. Maxwell, *The Big Bend of the Rio Grande,* 2008).

KEY INFORMATION

ADDRESS:	P. O. Box 2319 Presidio, TX 79845
OPERATED BY:	Texas Parks and Wildlife Department
INFORMATION:	(432) 229-3416
RESERVATIONS:	(512) 389-8900; www.tpwd.state.tx.us
OPEN:	All year
SITES:	2 (Grassy Banks), 4 (Colorado Canyon and Madera Canyon), 12 interior primitive sites
EACH SITE:	Table, shelter, fire ring
ASSIGNMENT:	Reservations get you in the campground; site choice is first come, first served
REGISTRATION:	Barton Warnock Education Center or Fort Leaton State Historic Site
FACILITIES:	Chemical toilets along the river
PARKING:	At each site
FEE:	$3 per person plus $8 camping fee
ELEVATION:	2,376 feet
RESTRICTIONS:	*Pets:* On leash only *Fires:* In fire rings only *Alcohol:* Prohibited *Vehicles:* 2 per site *Other:* Maximum 8 persons per site; guests must leave by 10 p.m.; quiet time 10 p.m.–6 a.m.; bring your own firewood or charcoal; limited supplies in Lajitas; pick up main supplies in Presidio; gathering firewood prohibited

MAP

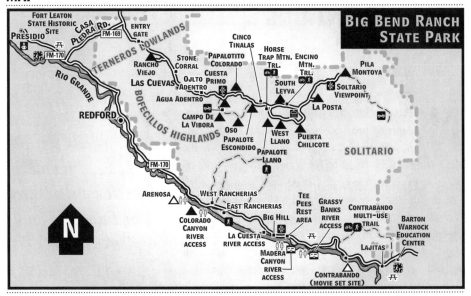

GETTING THERE

From Presidio, begin your trip 3 miles south on FM 170 at the Ft. Leaton State Historic site for registration, payment of fees, and information about weather conditions and site availability. From Lajitas and the ghost town of Terlingua, travel northwest on FM 170. The various sites are well marked along the road.

GPS COORDINATES

UTM Zone (WGS84) 13R
Easting 620562
Northing 3238572
Latitude N 29.2703°
Longitude W 103.7590°

6
DAVIS MOUNTAINS STATE PARK

NAMED AFTER HISTORIC Ft. Davis, the Davis Mountains provide a perfect home for this state park and tent campers seeking relief from the heat and humidity of other Texas campgrounds. Located at more than 5,000 feet, the campground stretches along the mostly dry Keesey Creek and is sheltered by a mixture of mature pine, juniper, and oak trees as well as the neighboring volcanic peaks. This 2,700-acre park was developed between 1933 and 1935 by the Civilian Conservation Corp., whose stone work remains intact and symbolizes workers grateful for even back-breaking employment during The Great Depression. One of the best examples is the Indian Lodge, completed in 1935. Now fully restored, it continues to serve travelers escaping the lowland heat or traveling to other, more remote parts of this dry and beautiful country.

The tent camping sites are located along Park Road 3 and begin just past the turnoff to RV sites 1 through 61. In order to select the best and most private tent camping areas, continue on Park Road 3, passing sites 62 through 67 until the Indian Lodge appears on your right. Turn left and cross the low water crossing of Keesey Creek to find sites 68 through 94, which will give you some excellent choices. Site 80, for example, is not only large, but has easy access to the bathroom and showers. Whichever tent site you choose, you will enjoy excellent shade trees and close proximity to Keesey Creek, which is dry most of the year, but do beware in heavy rainfall conditions. The campground is also sheltered by the towering Davis Mountains and surrounding rocky terrain, making for a wilderness experience in the high desert of West Texas.

While this campground appears quite civilized, the park advises you to beware of bears, mountain lions, and javelinas, and not to leave small children or pets unattended. It is also important to store your food

> *Whichever tent site you choose, you will enjoy excellent shade trees and close proximity to Keesey Creek.*

RATINGS

Beauty: ✪ ✪ ✪ ✪
Privacy: ✪ ✪ ✪
Spaciousness: ✪ ✪ ✪
Quiet: ✪ ✪ ✪
Security: ✪ ✪ ✪ ✪
Cleanliness: ✪ ✪ ✪ ✪

ADDRESS: P. O. Box 1707
TX Highway 118
N, Park Road 3
Ft. Davis, TX
79734

OPERATED BY: Texas Parks
and Wildlife
Department

INFORMATION: (432) 426-3337

RESERVATIONS: (512) 389-8900;
www.tpwd.state
.tx.us

OPEN: All year

SITES: 94

EACH SITE: Picnic table, fire
ring, water

ASSIGNMENT: Reservations get
you in the camp-
ground; site
choice is first
come, first served

REGISTRATION: At entrance
station

FACILITIES: Clean, modern
bathrooms

PARKING: At each site

FEE: $10 per night for
water-only camp-
sites; $4 per per-
son entrance fee

ELEVATION: 5,038 feet

RESTRICTIONS: *Pets:* On leash only
Fires: Charcoal
only
Alcohol: Prohibited
Vehicles: 2 per site
Other: Maximum 8
persons per site;
guests must leave
by 10 p.m.; quiet
time 10 p.m.–
6 a.m.; bring your
own charcoal;
limited supplies
available at park
store, located at
entrance station;
pick up other sup-
plies in Ft. Davis;
gathering fire-
wood prohibited

inside a closed vehicle to prevent attracting wild animals to the campground.

Besides the mild climate of the Davis Mountains,
the area also offers the vistas of Skyline Drive, which is
within the park and overlooks the town of Ft. Davis and
Ft. Davis National Historic Site, a must-see. This frontier
fort has a large number of buildings that have been
expertly restored. The visitor center and museum offer
a fascinating glimpse of Texas history and a chance to
learn not only about Native Americans who inhabited
this area, but also the famous "buffalo soldiers" who
were assigned to Ft. Davis after the Civil War.

After leaving the state park, turn left on Highway
118 and travel 14 miles to the internationally known
McDonald Observatory, which has hosted astronomers
since 1939. Its location on 6,791-foot Mt. Locke enjoys
the darkest skies in the continental United States, and
day and night tours are offered. While camping at Davis
Mountains State Park, be sure to attend a Star Party to
see heavenly sights a city dweller can only imagine.

RECOMMENDED READING

Black Frontiersman: The Memoirs of Henry O. Flipper by
Theodore D. Harris. Available at Ft. Davis National
Historic Site, this book chronicles the first black gradu-
ate of West Point and his assignment to Ft. Davis as one
of the famous "Buffalo Soldiers."

VOICES FROM THE CAMPFIRE

"As darkness falls, though, an even more spectacular
canvas unfolds overhead. The dark sky begins to blaze
with stars . . . And when the Milky Way arcs overhead,
it looks like a shimmering river of light" (*McDonald
Observatory Guide,* 2008).

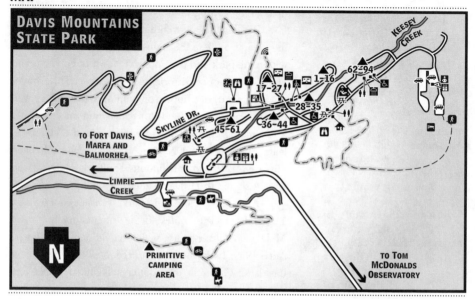

GETTING THERE

From Ft. Davis, go west 3 miles on Highway 118. Park entrance is on your left.

GPS COORDINATES

UTM Zone (WGS84)	13R
Easting	602672
Northing	3385695
Latitude	N 30.5994°
Longitude	W 103.9290°

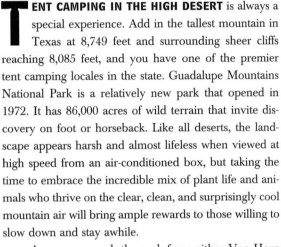

7
GUADALUPE MOUNTAINS NATIONAL PARK

> *Take the time to embrace the incredible mix of plant and animal life that thrives in this desert landscape.*

TENT CAMPING IN THE HIGH DESERT is always a special experience. Add in the tallest mountain in Texas at 8,749 feet and surrounding sheer cliffs reaching 8,085 feet, and you have one of the premier tent camping locales in the state. Guadalupe Mountains National Park is a relatively new park that opened in 1972. It has 86,000 acres of wild terrain that invite discovery on foot or horseback. Like all deserts, the landscape appears harsh and almost lifeless when viewed at high speed from an air-conditioned box, but taking the time to embrace the incredible mix of plant life and animals who thrive on the clear, clean, and surprisingly cool mountain air will bring ample rewards to those willing to slow down and stay awhile.

As you approach the park from either Van Horn or El Paso, the vast remoteness begins to sink in, and the first view of El Capitan's 2,000-foot-plus rock face brings easy comparisons to the more-famous Yosemite Valley monolith. The visitor center turnoff is on your left and provides the best place to start your visit. There is an excellent small museum and the rangers are glad to fill you in on the best hikes in the park and what conditions you will likely face in the backcountry. Note that the visitor center does not have supplies.

As with most national parks, you will need a backcountry permit for overnight stays, but day hikes are unrestricted. However, be sure to use the hiker's register at the trailhead so your absence might be noticed in a more timely manner should you stray, twist your ankle, or have an unscheduled meeting with a mountain lion or rattlesnake. Remember that 60 percent of this park has been designated official wilderness and must be respected as such.

Leaving the visitor center parking lot, Pine Springs Campground is on the right. The central parking lot contains the restrooms, marked RV spaces with

RATINGS

Beauty: ✿ ✿ ✿ ✿ ✿
Privacy: ✿ ✿ ✿
Spaciousness: ✿ ✿ ✿
Quiet: ✿ ✿ ✿ ✿
Security: ✿ ✿ ✿ ✿
Cleanliness: ✿ ✿ ✿ ✿

no hookups, and the trailhead (which leads to the strenuous, but spectacular, 8.4-mile Guadalupe Peak Trail, where you can truly say you have been to the top of Texas).

Upon returning to the parking lot, the tent-camping road starts on your immediate left with sites 4 through 12 a short walk from the parking spots. The other sites each have one parking spot. All sites are nicely spaced, with level tent pads and unrestricted views of the Guadalupe Mountains, which not only draw the eye but seem to beckon you to explore further. Two group sites are available for a minimum of 10 persons or maximum of 20. If you are lucky enough to be here during a full moon, its fiery orange appearance on the eastern horizon will help you understand the reverence paid the moon by the Mescalero Apaches, who thrived here until the European explorers decided to convert them to their own view of religion and civilization.

Leaving the tent-camping area, return to US 62/180 and turn left. Drive 0.3 miles and stop at The Pinery Butterfield Stage Ruins for a lesson on the real Old West. In 1858, this station acted as a true oasis for the passengers, drivers, and horses that were part of the first intercontinental mail route from St. Louis to San Francisco. The route was chosen to avoid the dangerous mountains to the north, but instead encroached on Indian territory to the south. It only lasted until the Civil War, but it remains a true monument to courage and endurance prior to the era of railroads, which replaced the stagecoach on this long and dangerous route.

Continuing on the main highway, travel north just under 7 miles until you reach the McKittrick Canyon turnoff on your left. This day-use area contains another must-see Texas trail. This 6.8-mile round-trip trail leads you deep into the park and a rich landscape that mixes prickly pear cacti and agaves with a canyon woodland of willows, alligator junipers, ponderosa pines, and the most beautiful Texas madrones, whose trunk and limbs turn almost red alongside the smooth, tan bark. This trail is rated moderate for a rough surface, but the persistent hiker will be rewarded for the effort. In the fall, the foliage explodes into colors even a Northeasterner can appreciate.

KEY INFORMATION

ADDRESS:	H.C. 60, Box 400 Salt Flat, Texas 79847
OPERATED BY:	National Park Service
INFORMATION:	(915) 828-3251
RESERVATIONS:	Group sites only at (915) 828-3251
OPEN:	All year
SITES:	20 (Pine Springs Campground)
EACH SITE:	Picnic table and level tent pad
ASSIGNMENT:	First come, first served
REGISTRATION:	At registration station
FACILITIES:	Modern restrooms with service sink but no showers; water
PARKING:	At each site except 4–12
FEE:	$8 per site, $4 per site with Golden Age Passport; $3 per person at group site, $1.50 per person with Golden Age Passport
ELEVATION:	5,707 feet
RESTRICTIONS:	*Pets:* On leash only; no pets on trails *Fires:* **Prohibited but containerized fuel stoves allowed** *Alcohol:* **Prohibited** *Vehicles:* **1 per site; 2 tents maximum** *Other:* **Maximum 6 persons per site; guests must leave by 8 p.m.; quiet time 8 p.m.–8a.m.; pick up supplies in El Paso, Van Horn, or Carlsbad; gathering firewood prohibited**

MAP

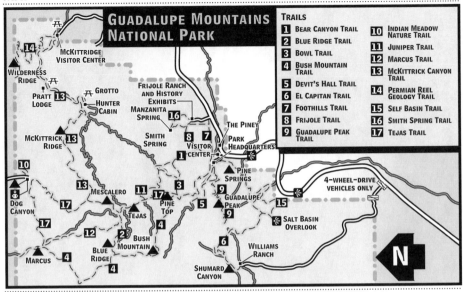

GUADALUPE MOUNTAINS NATIONAL PARK

McKittridge Visitor Center
Wilderness Ridge 14
Pratt Lodge 13
Grotto
Hunter Cabin
Frijole Ranch and History Exhibits
Manzanita Spring 16
McKittrick Ridge 13
Smith Spring 16
The Piney
Park Headquarters
8 7 Visitor Center 1
Pine Springs
Dog Canyon 10
Mescalero 13 11 17
Tejas 17
Pine Top 3
Guadalupe Peak 9 15
4-Wheel-Drive Vehicles Only
Salt Basin Overlook
Blue Ridge 12
Bush Mountain 2
Williams Ranch 6
Marcus 4
Shumard Canyon
N

TRAILS

1	Bear Canyon Trail	10	Indian Meadow Nature Trail
2	Blue Ridge Trail	11	Juniper Trail
3	Bowl Trail	12	Marcus Trail
4	Bush Mountain Trail	13	McKittrick Canyon Trail
5	Devit's Hall Trail	14	Permian Reel Geology Trail
6	El Capitan Trail	15	Self Basin Trail
7	Foothills Trail	16	Smith Spring Trail
8	Frijole Trail	17	Tejas Trail
9	Guadalupe Peak Trail		

GETTING THERE

From Van Horn, Texas, travel north 58 miles on TX 54. From Carlsbad, New Mexico, travel southwest 45 miles on US 62/180.

GPS COORDINATES

UTM Zone (WGS84)   13R
Easting   515991
Northing   3522647
Latitude   N 31.8394°
Longitude   W 104.8310°

A final stop will require a two-hour drive north into New Mexico past Carlsbad Caverns National Park on US 62/180, a left on Dark Canyon Road (CR 408), and another left on TX 137 until you reach Dog Canyon Campground. Here you'll find nine walk-in tent sites with drinking water, restrooms, and a ranger station. The elevation is 6,300 feet and will give you excellent access to the high country, including a secluded, forested canyon on this little-used north side of the park. Bring some good hiking boots and all your supplies to stay awhile in one of the least-known but truly wild tent camping spots in Texas.

RECOMMENDED READING

The Guadalupes by Dan Murphy. This small book gives a concise history of the area along with some great photographs. It's available at the visitor center.

VOICES FROM THE CAMPFIRE

"What draws us into the desert is the search for something intimate in the remote" (Edward Abbey, *A Voice Crying in the Wilderness*, 1989).

CENTRAL TEXAS AND
THE HILL COUNTRY

8
BASTROP AND BUESCHER STATE PARKS

LEAVING THE HISTORIC TOWN of Bastrop on TX 21, Bastrop State Park is a family-friendly destination with a surprisingly rugged side. As you enter the park, the golf course along the road is not your usual wilderness approach, but the towering loblolly pines in this central Texas location invite you in. Leaving the entrance station on Park Road 1A, the dining hall and swimming area is .3 miles straight ahead. This Civilian Conservation Corps (CCC)–built area is a National Historic Landmark and includes a large outdoor stone deck with smokers and grills for group reservations.

Turn left and then an immediate right toward campsites 1 through 42. Make another hard right into the day-use area or you will end up in the Piney Hill RV area. Back in the day-use area, the Deer Run Camping Area is past the playground and down a slight hill off a gravel road. Sites 36 through 42 are on the immediate right. Sites 31 through 35 are in the circular drive area and provide the most privacy for the tent camper, but still provide easy access to the modern restrooms and showers. The sites all back up to a heavily wooded area shaded by the towering Lost Pines Forest.

As you venture out into the park, you begin to feel like you have taken a trip to deep east Texas, even though you are 100 miles away from the similar Piney Woods region. This island of approximately 75,000 acres has persisted in the area for more than 18,000 years and has adapted to 30 percent less rainfall than its eastern Texas cousin. The park contains an extensive 11-trail system—including the 6.88-mile Lost Pines Trail—that has multiple elevation changes and allows primitive camping with a permit for the backpackers in your group. There is also a set of 12 historic cabins at the end of Park Road 1B for the less adventurous. Even if you aren't staying in the cabins, visit this area for the rustic architecture.

> *Slow down and enjoy this unique island of towering piney woods.*

RATINGS

Beauty: ☆ ☆ ☆ ☆
Privacy: ☆ ☆ ☆
Spaciousness: ☆ ☆ ☆
Quiet: ☆ ☆ ☆
Security: ☆ ☆ ☆ ☆
Cleanliness: ☆ ☆ ☆

KEY INFORMATION

ADDRESS: PO Box 518
Bastrop, TX 78602

OPERATED BY: Texas Parks
and Wildlife Dept.

INFORMATION: (512) 321-2101

RESERVATIONS: (512) 389-8900;
www.tpwd.state
.tx.us

OPEN: All year

SITES: 16 (Deer Run); 7
(Copperas Creek);
23 (Lakeview)

EACH SITE: Picnic table, fire
ring, lantern hook

ASSIGNMENT: Reservations get
you in the camp-
ground; site
choice is first
come, first served

REGISTRATION: At headquarters

FACILITIES: Restrooms, showers in RV area,
swimming pool,
golf course, park
store, dining hall
for groups

PARKING: At each site except
Copperas Creek

FEE: $12 water only;
$10 primitive site;
$4 per person
entrance fee

ELEVATION: 581 feet

RESTRICTIONS: *Pets:* On leash only
Fires: In fire rings
Alcohol: Prohibited
Vehicles: 2 per site
Other: Maximum 8
persons per site;
guests must leave
by 10 p.m.; quiet
time 10 p.m.–
6 a.m.; bring your
own firewood or
charcoal; limited
supplies at park
store; pick up
main supplies in
Bastrop; gather-
ing firewood
prohibited

Returning to the dining hall and swimming area, follow Park Road 1A to the Creekside Camping Area for walk-in sites 43 through 48. These primitive sites flank the 1.14-mile Scenic Overlook Trail and can also be accessed through the Copperas Creek RV Camping Area.

Whatever your interest—camping under the Lost Pines, hiking the challenging trail system, or just cruising scenic Park Road 1C to nearby Buescher State Park—Bastrop State Park is not to be missed.

As you leave Bastrop State Park on Park Road 1C, this little-known parkway will remind you of an earlier time when the CCC was busy building the infrastructure of our nation's parks. The road's steep grades will deter most RVs. It is a popular bicycle path, so be sure to share the road. These hilly 7.5 miles are shaded by a wide variety of oaks and those Lost Pines, and contain some low water crossings and a viewpoint to the right off a ridgeline.

As you reach the end of this Texas version of the Natchez Trace, the road dead-ends at the Lakeview Camping Area and sites 41 through 55. These nicely spaced sites start on the right and back up to a small creek area with huge moss-covered trees that provide much-needed summer shade. As you reach the circle and sites 46 through 49, you can see the 25-acre park lake and enjoy a small campground without the RV traffic. The tent sites are level and make an excellent base camp for bicycle trips or day hikes on the 7.7-mile Buescher Hiking Trail.

After site 49, look for the easy trail to walk-in sites 56 through 60 on the right. These well-hidden sites are just far enough off the road for campers to feel they have reached the wilderness without the exertion of a backpack. Central parking and the main pavilion are on the left along with modern restrooms and showers just ahead on the right. Returning to Park Road 1E, turn right up the hill to find the Buescher Hiking trailhead and parking for walk-in sites 61 through 65. These sites off the road are easily accessible, and campers won't find an RV in sight. If you get lost and end up in the Cozy Circle Camping Area, you will find a no-tents sign. I guess not so cozy for everyone.

MAP

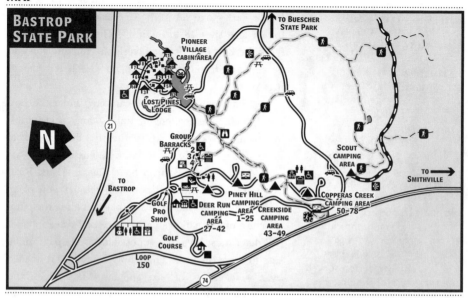

BASTROP STATE PARK

TO BUESCHER STATE PARK

PIONEER VILLAGE CABIN AREA

LOST PINES LODGE

N

TO BASTROP

GROUP BARRACKS

SCOUT CAMPING AREA

TO SMITHVILLE

GOLF PRO SHOP

DEER RUN CAMPING AREA 27–42

PINEY HILL CAMPING AREA 1–25

CREEKSIDE CAMPING AREA 43–49

COPPERAS CREEK CAMPING AREA 50–78

GOLF COURSE

LOOP 150

MAP

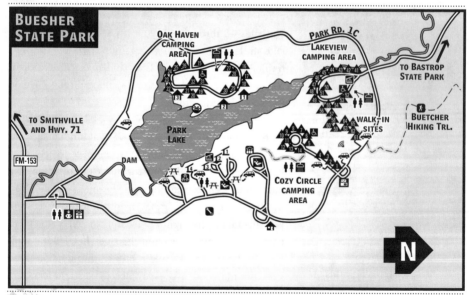

BUESHER STATE PARK

OAK HAVEN CAMPING AREA

PARK RD. 1C

LAKEVIEW CAMPING AREA

TO BASTROP STATE PARK

TO SMITHVILLE AND HWY. 71

BUETCHER HIKING TRL.

FM-153

PARK LAKE

DAM

WALK–IN SITES

COZY CIRCLE CAMPING AREA

N

Whichever tent site you do choose, this post oak–savannah region allows exploration of not only the famous Lost Pines, but also of endangered species, such as the Houston toad. There are also pileated woodpeckers here darting from tree to tree in their search for lunch or a nesting site.

RECOMMENDED READING

The Civilian Conservation Corps in Texas State Parks by James Wright Steely and Joseph R. Montione. Texas Parks and Wildlife Department, 1986.

VOICES FROM THE CAMPFIRE

"The foundations of the state park system enjoyed by Texans today were laid in the bittersweet years of the 1930s" (James Wright Steely, 1986).

GETTING THERE

BASTROP:

From Bastrop, travel east 0.9 miles on Highway 21. Turn right at the sign. Park entrance is on the immediate left.

BUESCHER:

From Bastrop State Park, Park Road 1C takes you to the Lakeview Campground. From TX 71, travel 2 miles north on FM 153 to Park Road 1 and the Buescher entrance station.

GPS COORDINATES

UTM Zone (WGS84)	14R
Easting	665074
Northing	3332213
Latitude	N 30.1100°
Longitude	W 97.2867°

9
LAKE BUCHANAN–
CANYON OF THE
EAGLES

AS YOU LEAVE **BURNET** **HEADING WEST** on TX 29, the Texas Hill Country views begin to unfold on the horizon. Turning right on FM 2341, this scenic winding road takes you away from civilization and dead-ends into Canyon of the Eagles. This multi-function park is part of the Lower Colorado River Authority (LCRA) system and provides a wide range of activities for the whole family.

As you enter the park on the Heart of Texas Wildlife Trail, the Eagle Eye Observatory turnoff is on your immediate right at 0.1 mile. This 0.8-mile gravel road leads to one of the darkest areas of the state and to a permanent observation area hosted by the Austin Astronomical Society. On most Friday and Sunday nights, the observatory's retractable roof is opened to the heavens and guests are able to peer through one of its large telescopes at such wonders as the rings of Jupiter or a spectacular double star.

Returning to the main road, the entrance to Chimney Slough Campsites is across the way. These 23 sites back up to a rugged, heavily wooded area, but are nicely spaced with sites 1 through 3 located at the end of the road for extra privacy.

Back on the paved park road, a left turn brings you to the Bird and Butterfly Trail, which is home to the endangered golden-cheeked warbler and black-capped vireo. Continue 0.5 miles past the lodge turnoff, and the central restrooms and showers are on the left along with the RV park where tent campers register with the park host.

Another .2 miles bring you to a fork in the road. To the right are the fishing pier and a group site for up to 50 campers. To the left are the Tanner Point Campground and 10 well-spaced tent sites connected by a rough gravel road. These primitive sites do not have water, but they do have a wilderness feel and sunset

If you want a wilderness-type experience, but need to bring along the less adventurous, Canyon of the Eagles is a perfect weekend destination.

RATINGS

Beauty: ✩ ✩ ✩ ✩
Privacy: ✩ ✩ ✩ ✩
Spaciousness: ✩ ✩ ✩ ✩
Quiet: ✩ ✩ ✩ ✩
Security: ✩ ✩ ✩ ✩
Cleanliness: ✩ ✩ ✩ ✩

ADDRESS:	Highway 2341 NE Lake Buchanan Burnet, TX 78611
OPERATED BY:	LCRA/Thousand Trails
INFORMATION:	(512) 715-0290 or (800) 977-0081; www.lcra.org/parks
RESERVATIONS:	(512) 389-8900; www.tpwd.state.tx.us
OPEN:	All year
SITES:	33
EACH SITE:	Picnic table, fire ring
ASSIGNMENT:	Reservations get you in the campground; site choice is first come, first served
REGISTRATION:	At camp host
FACILITIES:	Modern restrooms near lodge; portable toilets near tent sites
PARKING:	At or near each site
FEE:	$12 (Chimney Slough); $10 (Tanner Point); $5 per person entrance fee; $4 ages 65 and over
ELEVATION:	1,071 feet
RESTRICTIONS:	*Pets:* On leash only *Fires:* In fire rings *Alcohol:* Prohibited *Vehicles:* 2 per site *Other:* Maximum 8 persons per site; guests must leave by 10 p.m.; quiet time 10 p.m.–6 a.m.; bring your own firewood or charcoal; limited supplies at park store; pick up main supplies in Burnet

views that overcome any inconvenience of bringing in your own water or taking a short walk with your gear. The sounds of the birds and a cool breeze off the lake make these sites a must-stop.

Returning to the main paved road, a right turn toward the dock takes you .1 mile to one of the park's main attractions. Here passengers board the 70-foot *Texas Eagle* for the two-hour scenic Vanishing Texas River Cruise up the Colorado River Canyon. The canyon's shores have been allowed to remain wild and offer an outdoor experience hard to duplicate in these days of waterfront developments. In the late fall and winter, these boat trips are very popular due to sightings of American bald eagles, which make this their winter home. Reservations are recommended at (800) 4-RIVER-4 or www.vtrc.com.

As you head out of the park, don't miss the lodge area, which has great views of Lake Buchanan, a restaurant, and cozy cabins for nontent campers. There is also live entertainment on the patio on many weekends. If you are looking for a wilderness-type experience, but need to bring along the less adventurous, then Canyon of the Eagles is a perfect weekend destination.

However, if less civilization is your goal, return to TX 29, turn right, and make another right on FM 261. FM 261 follows the west shore of Lake Buchanan, and the Black Rock Park entrance is on the right at 2.7 miles. The friendly park hosts will greet you and assist with site selection, starting with sites 1 through 3 on your immediate right. These lakefront sites are well spaced and have excellent views of the massive Lake Buchanan. Continuing on the main park road, sites 4 through 11 are on your left and are slightly elevated for grand views of the lake. Site 6 is especially large with two grills and two tables. Sites 7 through 9 also have large shade trees for an afternoon retreat from the summer sun. Site 12 is a solo site facing east on the right near the lake, while site 13 is on the peninsula facing a sandy beach to the west. Sites 19 and 20 have huge oak trees and lake views.

While camping at Black Rock Park, keep a sharp lookout not only for great blue herons and red-tailed hawks soaring high above the lake, but also for American white pelicans and bald eagles. This area is also home to the endangered golden-cheeked warblers and black-capped vireos. Overall, this family-friendly park is a great spot to relax, throw in a fishing line, or just enjoy the serenity of Lake Buchanan just a few steps from your tent.

As you leave the park entrance, a right turn will take you to the adjacent Llano County Park and a public boat ramp. Continue north 6.9 miles to the historic Bluffton Store and make a right turn on RR 2241 for 7.3 miles. The Fall Creek Winery is on your right and schedules festivals and events, such as a grape stomp, throughout the year.

Returning 3.2 miles on the main road, turn left on FM 3014 and take another left at 0.4 miles into the Cedar Point Recreation/Resource Area. This unimproved and primitive camping area has no numbered sites, but several gravel turnoffs lead to the water's edge on both sides of the peninsula. If you go to the end of the road, you arrive at a perfect waterfront site with 180-degree views of the lake and access to swimming or boating. While this site has no restrooms, showers, tables, or drinking water, it is a great getaway for those tent campers looking to leave civilization behind, even for just one night.

RECOMMENDED READING

Canyon of the Eagles: A History of Lake Buchanan and Official Guide to the Vanishing Texas River Cruise by C. L. Yarbrough.

VOICES FROM THE CAMPFIRE

"In the ultimate democracy of time, Henry Thoreau has outlived his contemporaries. . . . The deeper our United States sinks into industrialism, urbanism, militarism . . . the more poignant, strong, and appealing becomes Thoreau's demand for the right of every man, every woman, every child, every dog, every tree, every snail darter, every lousewort, every living thing, to live its own life in its own way at its own pace in its own square mile of home. Or in its own stretch of river" (Edward Abbey, *Down the River with Henry Thoreau,* 1981).

MAP

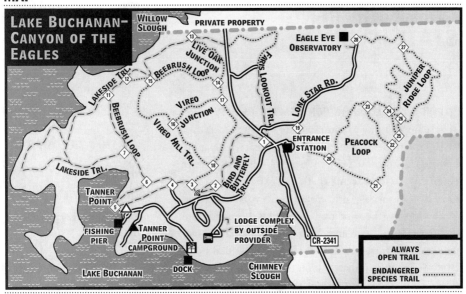

GETTING THERE

Travel 2.7 miles west of Burnet on TX 29 and turn right on FM 2341. The park is 15.4 miles at the road's end.

GPS COORDINATES

UTM Zone (WGS84)   14R
Easting   554300
Northing   3416907
Latitude   N 30.8842°
Longitude   W 98.4319°

IF YOU ARE LOOKING FOR REMOTE BEAUTY and a rare opportunity to camp next to a major river, then Colorado Bend State Park is a great destination. Leaving Llano on TX 16, you travel north 18.4 miles on one of the most scenic roads in Texas into the small town of Cherokee. Turn east (right) on Ranch Road 501 and follow the winding road until it dead-ends into FM 580. Turn right and follow the Colorado River until the road turns into County Road 436 at Bad Bob's Bend Store. Pick up last-minute supplies and proceed toward this under-visited tent camper's paradise. The road has several low-water crossings with open range land on both sides. It becomes a well-graded gravel road for about 8 miles, and you know you are headed off the beaten path. Watch for deer and enjoy the rough terrain of cactus and rocks until you pass the park boundary. You'll see the Windmill Trail on your right at 1.2 miles and a great Hill Country view at 4.5 miles, just prior to the return of pavement and a steep descent to park headquarters and the Colorado River. Check in with the park rangers at this remote outpost and get assistance with your campsite selection.

Sites 23 through 38 are to your right and numbered parking spaces are to your left. The campsites are down a small embankment and spread on a large, grassy knoll next to the Colorado River. Look for riverside site 30 under a large clump of willow trees, or site 38 under a huge pecan tree. All these sites have river views, and a massive rock wall on the other side hides the campground from the outside world.

Continue on the main park road toward the group campground and day-use area. Look for the Spicewood Springs trailhead at the end of the parking lot and follow the tree-lined path to a series of small pools and waterfalls as they cascade down the hillside. The trail also heads uphill, and at the top, you leave the "tourist"

> *Be sure to visit the spring-fed waterfall in this spectacular Hill Country setting.*

RATINGS

Beauty: ✿ ✿ ✿
Privacy: ✿ ✿ ✿
Spaciousness: ✿ ✿ ✿ ✿
Quiet: ✿ ✿ ✿ ✿
Security: ✿ ✿ ✿ ✿
Cleanliness: ✿ ✿ ✿

ADDRESS:	P.O. Box 118 Bend, TX 76824
OPERATED BY:	Texas Parks and Wildlife Dept.
INFORMATION:	(800) 792-1112 or (915) 628-3240
RESERVATIONS:	(512) 389-8900; www.tpwd.state .tx.us
OPEN:	All year
SITES:	38
EACH SITE:	Central water, picnic table, fire pit, lantern hook
ASSIGNMENT:	Reservations get you in the campground; site choice is first come, first served
REGISTRATION:	At headquarters
FACILITIES:	Park store, chemical toilets, kayak rentals
PARKING:	At each site; short walk to riverside sites
FEE:	$14 drive-in sites 8–22; $12 riverbank walk-in sites 1–7, 23–38; $3 per person entrance fee ages 13 up; under age 13 free
ELEVATION:	1,069 feet
RESTRICTIONS:	*Pets:* On leash only *Fires:* In fire pits *Alcohol:* Prohibited *Vehicles:* 2 per site *Other:* Maximum 8 persons per site; guests must leave by 10 p.m.; quiet time 10 p.m.– 6 a.m.; bring your own firewood or charcoal; limited supplies at park store; pick up main supplies in Llano or San Saba

area and start into some real wilderness. Watch for Texas-size red ants and silver dollar–size spiders that seem to like to spin their symmetrical webs between the junipers and directly across the trail. Luckily, it's easy to go around these scary-looking friends, but don't forget to check the trail ahead for the far-more-dangerous diamondback rattlesnakes as they wait in the shade or come out in the cool of the evening after the hot Texas sun heads toward the horizon.

If you happen upon any of these vipers, give them a wide berth and head quickly back to the campground and peaceful riverside sites 1 through 15. Sites 5 through 7 are near the composting toilet, and Site 7 is a large, private site near enough to hear the river. Site 14 has the shade of a giant pecan tree. Sites 16 through 22 are away from the river, but have the protection of a rock escarpment and nice tree cover. They also allow close-in parking.

As you enjoy the camping, don't miss the chance to rent kayaks or take the Saturday-only guided tour to Gorman Falls. The $5-per-person cost is well worth the chance to see a spring-fed waterfall in a spectacular Hill Country setting. It's a 1.5-mile round-trip walk, so bring your water and camera for a special treat to finish off your visit to this remote location.

There is also weekend access to Wild Cave and Gorman Cave, but be sure to make reservations at (325) 628-3240.

RECOMMENDED READING

Beyond the Hundredth Meridian: John Wesley Powell and the Second Opening of the West by Wallace Stegner, 1953, 1954, 1992.

VOICES FROM THE CAMPFIRE

"We are now ready to start on our way down the Great Unknown . . . We have an unknown distance yet to run; an unknown river yet to explore. What falls there are, we know not; what rocks beset the channel, we know not; what walls rise over the river, we know not" (John Wesley Powell, 1869, as he entered the Grand Canyon).

MAP

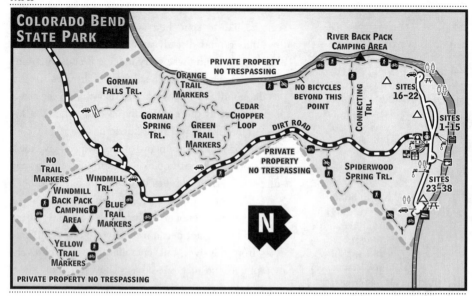

GETTING THERE

From San Saba, travel 19 miles on Highway 190 East and FM 580 south to Bend. Take CR 436 south 10 miles to park headquarters on your right.

GPS COORDINATES

UTM Zone (WGS84)	14R
Easting	553210
Northing	3432229
Latitude	N 31.0225°
Longitude	W 98.4425°

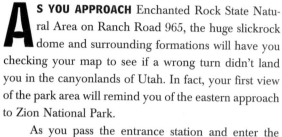

> *The huge slickrock dome will have you wondering if a wrong turn didn't land you in the canyonlands of Utah.*

AS YOU APPROACH Enchanted Rock State Natural Area on Ranch Road 965, the huge slickrock dome and surrounding formations will have you checking your map to see if a wrong turn didn't land you in the canyonlands of Utah. In fact, your first view of the park area will remind you of the eastern approach to Zion National Park.

As you pass the entrance station and enter the park, the RVs and trailers are diverted into a parking lot on the left, while the tent campers and day hikers cross over a wide low-water crossing into the main camping area. Sites 1 through 3 are on your immediate right and provide shelter and close-in parking, but also the most road traffic. Continuing to the right past these sites toward the day-use area, the parking for sites 35 through 46 is on your left. These sites are a short walk into the trees toward Enchanted Rock and will give you excellent access to the summit trail.

Returning back toward sites 1 through 3, the modern bathrooms and showers are on your left, along with tent sites 4 through 20. These nicely spaced sites are set back from the road for a little extra quiet. Sites 17, 19, and 21 are the most private and back up to Sandy Creek. These sites also provide an excellent vantage point to view Enchanted Rock and the surrounding rugged landscape.

Returning to the parking area, the other side of the road will allow close-in access to some of the premier campsites in Texas. A short walk across wooden bridges will lead you into a heavily wooded area and sites 23 through 34. These sites are well spaced and divided by underbrush and rocky ravines. The white-tailed deer scurry between the tents, and you'll immediately feel a sense of peacefulness. There is also a sense of grandeur looming just a few feet away as these sites nestle close to the smooth sandstone monolith that

RATINGS

Beauty: ✪ ✪ ✪ ✪
Privacy: ✪ ✪ ✪ ✪
Spaciousness: ✪ ✪ ✪ ✪
Quiet: ✪ ✪ ✪ ✪
Security: ✪ ✪ ✪ ✪
Cleanliness: ✪ ✪ ✪

makes this park a popular stop for all Texas travelers visiting the Hill Country.

After you pitch your tent, put on hiking boots or good sturdy tennis shoes and head to the Summit trailhead located at the end of the day-use parking lot. This short, 0.6-mile trail climbs a steep 425 feet, but is well worth the effort. Be sure not to hurry, but enjoy the panoramic views along with the hearty cactus and juniper appearing to grow out of solid rock. Take plenty of water and a bit of food so you can stay and ponder the beauty laid out before you.

Returning to the campground, the Loop Trail is a very nice 4-mile walk that will take you around the rock and to the primitive camping areas. There are also excellent opportunities to practice your rock-climbing skills, but registration with park headquarters is required.

As you leave the park, allow sufficient time to enjoy Fredericksburg, one of Texas's great Hill Country towns. The main street is lined with historic storefronts. The National Museum of the Pacific War has been updated and expanded to truly honor native Texan Admiral Chester Nimitz.

The other famous attraction that cannot be missed is the spring wildflower season. Perennial Texas natives, including multicolored bluebonnets, Indian paintbrush, and Indian blanket, cover roadsides and field after field. Mix in the flowering cactus and the awesome sight of Enchanted Rock and you quickly understand the irresistible lure of the Texas Hill Country.

RECOMMENDED READING

The Wild Muir: Twenty-two of John Muir's Greatest Adventures. Selected and introduced by Lee Stetson, 1994.

VOICES FROM THE CAMPFIRE

"Tell me what you will of the benefactions of city civilization. . . . I know that our bodies were made to thrive only in pure air, and the scenes in which pure air is found. If the death exhalations that brood the broad towns in which we so fondly compact ourselves were made visible, we should flee as from a plague" (John Muir, *John of the Mountains: The Unpublished Journals of John Muir,* 1938).

ADDRESS:	16710 Ranch Road 965 Fredericksburg, TX 78624-6554
OPERATED BY:	Texas Parks and Wildlife Dept.
INFORMATION:	(915) 247-3903
RESERVATIONS:	(512)389-8900; www.tpwd.state .tx.us
OPEN:	All year
SITES:	46
EACH SITE:	Picnic table, fire pit, lantern hook, water
ASSIGNMENT:	Reservations get you in the campground; site choice is first come, first served
REGISTRATION:	At entrance station/headquarters
FACILITIES:	Centrally located modern restrooms and showers
PARKING:	Central lots
FEE:	$15 per tent site with water; $6 per adult entrance fee, $3 ages 65 and older, ages 12 and under free
ELEVATION:	1,389 feet
RESTRICTIONS:	*Pets:* On leash only *Fires:* In fire pits *Alcohol:* Prohibited *Vehicles:* 2 per site *Other:* Maximum 8 persons per site; guests must leave by 10 p.m.; quiet time 10 p.m.– 6 a.m.; bring your own firewood or charcoal; limited supplies at park store; pick up main supplies in Fredericksburg or Llano; gathering firewood prohibited

MAP

GETTING THERE

From Fredericksburg, go
north on Ranch Road 965
for 17 miles. The park
entrance is on your left.

GPS COORDINATES

UTM Zone (WGS84)   14R
Easting   517245
Northing   3373740
Latitude   N 30.4958°
Longitude   W 98.8203°

YOU CAN TELL A PARK IS POPULAR when the drive-up to the entrance station has traffic lanes similar to a sports arena or a large amusement park. There is also a radio frequency for current information about this rather remote, but special, place. As you enter the park, be sure to get the extensive and detailed map to assist you in finding your campsite and begin exploring why Garner State Park has such a high number of visitors.

After leaving the entrance station, proceed 0.5 miles and turn left at the intersection toward Persimmon Hill Camping Area and sites 200 through 234. These sites enjoy adequate tree cover, and even-numbered sites 200 through 214 on your right back up to a steep cliff and your first views of the Rio Frio. This spring-fed river flows gently through the rolling terrain of the Texas Hill Country and provides a genuine oasis to Texans looking for summer relief. As the name of the river aptly describes, the water is wonderfully cool even on the hottest afternoon. Look for sites 204 and 210 to have the best river views, but do be careful of the cliff if out wandering at night. As an added bonus, there are central bathrooms with showers for the Persimmon Hill tent campers.

Returning to the main road, proceed past the Live Oak RV area and turn left into the Rio Frio Camping Area. Stay to the left after passing the sand volleyball court and continue down the hill to sites 467 through 444. There is parking at each site and the river is on your left about 50 yards away. The river is obscured by heavy brush, but numerous trails lead through the sand dunes to the gently flowing water. On a quiet night, or while enjoying an early cup of tea or coffee, you can hear the flowing ripples. You can also hear the rumble of nearby thunderstorms, which is a reminder to heed any warnings from the park

> *This spring-fed river provides a genuine oasis to Texans looking for summer relief.*

RATINGS

Beauty: ☆ ☆ ☆ ☆
Privacy: ☆ ☆ ☆
Spaciousness: ☆ ☆ ☆
Quiet: ☆ ☆ ☆
Security: ☆ ☆ ☆
Cleanliness: ☆ ☆ ☆

ADDRESS:	HCR 70, Box 599 Concan, TX 78838
OPERATED BY:	Texas Parks and Wildlife Dept.
INFORMATION:	(800) 792-1112; (830) 232-6132
RESERVATIONS:	(512) 389-8900; www.tpwd.state.tx.us
OPEN:	All year
SITES:	87 at Pecan Grove, 34 at Persimmon Hill, 56 at Rio Frio
EACH SITE:	Picnic table, fire ring, lantern hook, water
ASSIGNMENT:	Reservations get you in the campground, but first come, first served on site choice
REGISTRATION:	At headquarters
FACILITIES:	Modern bathrooms and showers, visitor center, sand volleyball courts, trails
PARKING:	At each site
FEE:	$10–$15 per night depending on location and date; $6 per person entrance fee
ELEVATION:	1,413 feet
RESTRICTIONS:	*Pets:* On leash only *Fires:* In fire rings *Alcohol:* Prohibited *Vehicles:* 2 per site *Other:* Maximum 8 persons per site; guests must leave by 10 p.m.; quiet time 10 p.m.– 6 a.m.; bring your own firewood or charcoal; limited supplies at park store or Leakey; pick up main supplies in Uvalde or Utopia

rangers. While the spring-fed water's level is fairly constant, heavy rainfall upstream can send this serene river into a massive flash flood that cleans and rearranges the sandbars for the next visitors.

At the river, you will find not only sandy beaches and gentle wading areas but also deep swimming holes and towering cypress trees with ropes to swing out on. Even if you are not climbing the big trees for a high dive, just watching Garner's visitors will conjure up an earlier time when going swimming for generations of Americans meant a lake, a river, or an ocean.

Returning to the main road, go past the River Crossing Camp Area and follow the signs to the day-use area and the pavilion. This drive will take you back up the hill for a great view of the entire park. As you descend, the Pecan Grove Camping Area is straight ahead, with some 87 water-only sites. They are shaded by huge pecan trees and are close to the most popular day-use areas, including swimming and paddleboats. These sites are good for families wishing to stay close to activities, but probably a little too busy for tent campers seeking solitude. Continuing past the day-use area, the pavilion is on your right. This fine stone structure was constructed by the Civilian Conservation Corps between 1935 and 1941. It contains a large dance floor and still hosts entertainment for all ages during the year.

As you enjoy the park's 9 miles of hiking trails, watch for the native white-tailed deer, Rio Grande turkeys, and even endangered species such as the golden-cheeked warbler and the black-capped vireo. There is also an occasional Texas jackrabbit just to remind you where you are and the harsh environment which surrounds this true oasis in the hills.

RECOMMENDED READING

The Adventures of Tom Sawyer by Mark Twain, 1876.

VOICES FROM THE CAMPFIRE

"It was the cool gray dawn, and there was a delicious sense of repose and peace in the deep pervading calm and silence of the woods. Not a leaf stirred; not a sound obtruded upon great Nature's meditation" (Mark Twain, 1876).

MAP

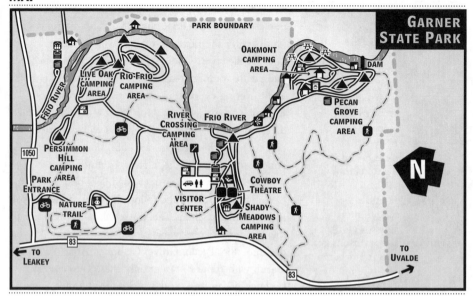

GETTING THERE

From US 90 and Uvalde,
take TX 83 north 31 miles to
FM 1050. Turn right and
drive 2 miles to Park Road
29. Turn right into the park.

GPS COORDINATES

UTM Zone (WGS84)	14R
Easting	428023
Northing	3274605
Latitude	N 29.5992°
Longitude	W 99.7433°

> *Wagon Ford Walk-in Tent Area provides some of the best tent camping you will find.*

LOCATED ONLY **30** MILES NORTH of San Antonio and 13 miles east of Boerne, this popular and scenic park is a must-stay camping stop. Be sure to start your wilderness adventure by picking up vital supplies at the Bear Moon Bakery and Café in historic downtown Boerne. Loaded with enough pastries and baked goods for the weekend, travel east on TX 46, turning north on Park Road 31 for 3.2 miles to the park headquarters, where the friendly rangers will assist you in selecting the best available site.

At 1.3 miles, stop at the entrance to the Honey Creek State Natural Area. Guided tours are the only access to this pristine watershed. Scheduled at 9 a.m. on Saturdays, these tours take you into a fragile ecosystem of centuries-old cypress trees, ancient oaks, pecans, walnuts, cedar elms, and ash juniper trees, where the endangered golden-cheeked warbler finds a sheltered habitat.

Continuing on the main road for 0.1 miles, turn left into Cedar Sage Camping Area, sites 1 through 37. Your first right turn will take you to sites 6 through 13, which have nice spacing and tree cover. Sites 9, 8, and 6 back up to a heavily wooded canyon for a little wilderness feel and extra privacy. Sites 1 through 5 are along the road, but are well spaced. Traveling toward the back of the campground, sites 16 through 19, 26, 29, and the 30s are also very acceptable large spaces. These sites even come with an efficient and cost-effective cleanup crew of red-headed turkey vultures, in case you forget to secure your food supplies.

Returning to the main park road, turn left and head down the hill toward the popular and usually crowded day-use area, but watch for an unassuming gravel road to your right at 0.3 miles. This turn into Wagon Ford Walk-In Tent Area offers some of the best tent camping you will find. Travel the 0.2 miles to the central parking area and take your gear to any one of 9

RATINGS

Beauty: ✪ ✪ ✪ ✪
Privacy: ✪ ✪ ✪
Spaciousness: ✪ ✪ ✪
Quiet: ✪ ✪ ✪
Security: ✪ ✪ ✪
Cleanliness: ✪ ✪ ✪

sites, which are all secluded in a grove of huge pecan trees. The trail is level and the farthest site is less than a 10-minute walk. As a bonus, sites 90 through 93 are close enough to hear the river, but high enough on the bank for relative safety from the unpredictable Guadalupe River below. Even so, always heed the ranger's advice if Texas thunderstorms are booming in the area. There is a steep, unofficial trail to the river, but it is better to follow the nature trail toward the day-use area, enjoying the multitude of birds and Spanish moss on the trees. No matter which of these sites you get to choose, bring your rolling ice chest and stay awhile.

Returning to the paved park road, a right turn brings you to a large parking lot and the main attraction. This heavily treed day-use area sits on the banks of one of Texas' most scenic rivers, the Guadalupe. With its cool and clear water ideal for family play, the backdrop of massive limestone cliffs blocks out the other world for a relaxing afternoon of picnicking and wading. Be sure to bring a swimsuit, sunscreen, and water shoes, along with an old-fashioned picnic lunch, to get full enjoyment of this natural wonder, but also be alert to the signs of flash flood if weather threatens.

Even on a crowded summer day, the sheer beauty of this stretch of river is sufficient to allow true relaxation. Best of all, your campsite at Wagon Ford gives you first choice of where to spend that day.

RECOMMENDED READING

Blue Highways: A Journey Into America by William Least Heat-Moon, 1982.

VOICES FROM THE CAMPFIRE

"I come more and more to the conclusion that wilderness, in America or anywhere else, is the only thing left that is worth saving. . . . God Bless America. Let's save some of it" (Edward Abbey, *A Voice Crying in the Wilderness, 1989*).

KEY INFORMATION

ADDRESS:	3350 Park Road 31 Spring Branch, TX 78070
OPERATED BY:	Texas Parks and Wildlife Dept.
INFORMATION:	(830)438-2656
RESERVATIONS:	(512)389-8900; www.tpwd.state .tx.us
OPEN:	All year
SITES:	37 in Cedar Sage; 9 in Wagon Ford
EACH SITE:	Picnic table, fire ring, lantern hook
ASSIGNMENT:	Reservations get you in the campground; site choice is first come, first served
REGISTRATION:	At headquarters
FACILITIES:	Modern restrooms and showers at Cedar Sage; compost toilets at Wagon Ford
PARKING:	At each site in Cedar Ridge; central parking at Wagon Ford
FEE:	$14–$16 per night; $6 per person entrance fee, ages 12 and under free
ELEVATION:	1,249 feet
RESTRICTIONS:	*Pets:* On leash only *Fires:* In fire rings *Alcohol:* Prohibited *Vehicles:* 2 per site *Other:* Maximum 8 persons per site; guests must leave by 10 p.m.; quiet time 10 p.m.– 6 a.m.; bring your own firewood or charcoal; limited supplies at park store; pick up main supplies in Boerne or San Antonio

MAP

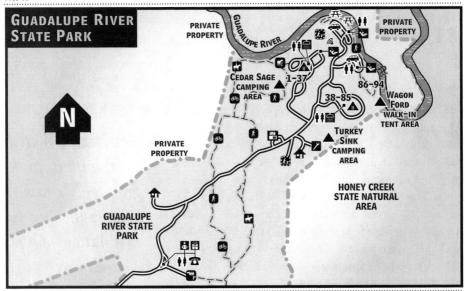

GETTING THERE

Drive 13 miles east of
Boerne on TX 46. Turn left
on Park Road 31 and drive
3.2 miles to the park
entrance.

GPS COORDINATES

UTM Zone (WGS84)   14R
Easting   547870
Northing   3302633
Latitude   N 29.8533°
Longitude   W 98.5044°

14
INKS LAKE
STATE PARK

LOCATED IN THE HEART of the Texas Hill Country approximately one hour from Austin, this popular state park still manages to give the tent camper a bit of solitude and relaxation. A caveat: avoid the RV and day-use areas on summer weekends, when the cool water acts as a magnet to every overheated Texan within driving distance. This is most evident in the Devil's Waterhole area, where the pink granite–like rock outcroppings provide natural diving platforms for the young at heart and brave to test their nerve. While you may share this area with a small crowd, the unique beauty of this classic swimming hole makes the visit well worth the effort.

You'll find tent sites 243 through 248 along the short trail to Devil's Waterhole. This nicely shaded group of sites provides easy access to the swimming area, which is far less crowded (almost no one) at dawn, sunset, or when the first cool weather drives the summer crowd back to town.

Returning to the opposite end of the park, follow the map to tent sites 300 through 349. This rugged and hilly area is divided into several loops, giving the sites a feeling of spaciousness and some privacy, especially on weekdays. On your immediate right, 300 through 304, which have level pads, make a great area for a group. Look for 304 to be nearest the water.

After another 0.3 miles on the main road, you'll reach sites 308 through 316. They're close to the restrooms and showers, with 311, 314, and 317 providing waterfront views and access for swimming or launching your canoe or kayak. There is nice tree cover and some brushy vegetation dividing these premium spots.

Continuing on the main road, sites 318 through 328 are on a rocky hillside to the left, but a right turn at 0.2 miles takes you to premium sites 332 through 334, which have easy water access. Also in this area, you'll

> *The Devil's Waterhole area, with its pink granite–like rock outcroppings, is the perfect destination on a hot summer day.*

RATINGS

Beauty: ☆ ☆ ☆
Privacy: ☆ ☆
Spaciousness: ☆ ☆ ☆
Quiet: ☆ ☆
Security: ☆ ☆ ☆
Cleanliness: ☆ ☆ ☆

KEY INFORMATION

ADDRESS: 3630 Park Road 4 West
Burnet, TX 78611

OPERATED BY: Texas Parks and Wildlife Dept.

INFORMATION: (512)793-2223

RESERVATIONS: (512)389-8900;
www.tpwd.state.tx.us

OPEN: All year

SITES: 56 tent-only sites

EACH SITE: Picnic table, fire ring, lantern hook

ASSIGNMENT: Reservations get you in the campground; site choice is first come, first served

REGISTRATION: Park headquarters

FACILITIES: Modern restrooms and showers, 2 fishing piers, golf course

PARKING: At each site except 244 and 246

FEE: $12 per night, water only; $5 per person entrance fee

ELEVATION: 928 feet

RESTRICTIONS: *Pets:* On leash only
Fires: In fire rings
Alcohol: Prohibited
Vehicles: 2 per site, except 1 car only at sites 245–248
Other: Maximum 8 persons per site; guests must leave by 10 p.m.; quiet time 10 p.m.–6 a.m.; bring your own firewood or charcoal; limited supplies at park store; pick up main supplies in Burnet; gathering firewood prohibited

find extra-large site 330, with two picnic tables. At 0.3 miles, look for the modern restrooms and showers and the park host (where you can purchase firewood) on the left, and then sites 339-343 on your right. Sites 341 and 342 are premium waterfront sites that have tree cover sufficient for hot afternoons.

With the fishing pier on your left, the final loop contains premium lakefront sites 346 through 348, which also have nice views of the lake.

As you would expect, all these lakefront sites get claimed early, so check in at headquarters first. Then you can head to the water, the well-stocked park store, or visit nearby Longhorn Cavern State Park, where its 68-degree year-round temperature and guided tours are the perfect addition to your camping weekend (or week) at Inks Lake.

RECOMMENDED READING

Wilderness and the American Mind by Roderick Nash, 1967.

VOICES FROM THE CAMPFIRE

"We are a great people because we have been so successful in developing and using our marvelous natural resources, but also, we Americans are the people we are largely because we have had the influence of the wilderness on our lives" (Congressman John P. Saylor as quoted by Roderick Nash, 1956).

MAP

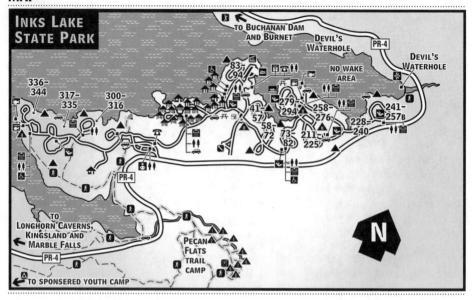

GETTING THERE

From Burnet drive 9 miles west on TX 29. Turn left on Park Road 4 and drive 3.4 miles before taking a right turn into the park.

GPS COORDINATES

UTM Zone (WGS84)	14R
Easting	560309
Northing	3400592
Latitude	N 30.7367°
Longitude	W 98.3700°

15
MCKINNEY FALLS
STATE PARK

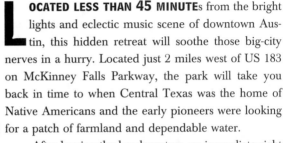

Watch for mule deer out for a late-afternoon snack and return often to this urban oasis.

LOCATED LESS THAN **45** MINUTEs from the bright lights and eclectic music scene of downtown Austin, this hidden retreat will soothe those big-city nerves in a hurry. Located just 2 miles west of US 183 on McKinney Falls Parkway, the park will take you back in time to when Central Texas was the home of Native Americans and the early pioneers were looking for a patch of farmland and dependable water.

After leaving the headquarters, an immediate right turn leads 0.4 miles to Lower McKinney Falls parking area and trailhead. From here, an easy five-minute walk takes you to one of the area's most-popular warm-weather destinations. The open expanses of smooth limestone and emerald-green pools invite swimming, wading, or just enjoying the small waterfall. Of course, this area can quickly change its character if thunderstorms are booming on the horizon. This area also marks the beginning of the 2.8-mile Homestead Trail for hikers and mountain bikers. As you leave the Lower Falls area, also note the parking on your right for the Picnic Trail day-use area for a little privacy off the paved road.

Returning to the main road, another right turn for 0.3 miles leads to the Upper McKinney Falls and the Smith Visitor Center and Viewpoint. This scenic part of the park is very popular, with access to the 1-mile Rock Shelter Interpretive Trail and the 2.8-mile Onion Creek Hike and Bike Trail, which circles the various campgrounds.

Following the main road to the right from the visitor center for 0.4 miles, turn right into the Walk-in Primitive Camping Area and the modern restrooms. This unassuming entrance quickly leads down a short incline to the Onion Creek Hike and Bike Trail, with towering shade trees along the creek bank. To the right are picnic areas. To the left are eight premium waterfront tent sites with a sense of relaxation far removed

RATINGS

Beauty: ✿ ✿ ✿ ✿
Privacy: ✿ ✿ ✿
Spaciousness: ✿ ✿ ✿
Quiet: ✿ ✿ ✿
Security: ✿ ✿ ✿ ✿
Cleanliness: ✿ ✿ ✿ ✿

from the nearby big city. Look for sites 2, 4, 5, and 8 for the most-level tent pads. Also, bring your bike or walking shoes, since the Onion Creek Trail is just a few steps away.

Back on the main road for 0.2 miles, the Shelter Area and Youth Group Area are on your right and the Grapevine Loop Camping (trailer/RV area) is another 0.1 mile. While this area is not ideal for tent camping, look for sites 41 through 84, as many of these have large, level tent pads next to the parking spots and would certainly be better than missing out on this fine state park.

As you leave, watch for mule deer out for a late-afternoon snack, and return often to this urban oasis.

RECOMMENDED READING

Words for the Wild: The Sierra Club Trailside Reader by Ann Ronald, 1987.

VOICES FROM THE CAMPFIRE

". . . Let me say a word or two in favor of the habit of keeping a journal of one's thoughts and days. . . . It is a sort of deposit account wherein one saves up bits and fragments of his life that would otherwise be lost to him" (John Burroughs, 1837–1921, as quoted by Ann Ronald).

KEY INFORMATION

ADDRESS:	5808 McKinney Falls Parkway Austin, TX 78744
OPERATED BY:	Texas Parks and Wildlife Dept.
INFORMATION:	(512) 243-1643
RESERVATIONS:	(512) 389-8900; www.tpwd.state.tx.us
OPEN:	All year
SITES:	8 tent-only; 81 with water and electricity
EACH SITE:	Picnic table, fire ring, lantern ring
ASSIGNMENT:	Reservations get you in the campground; site choice is first come, first served
REGISTRATION:	At headquarters
FACILITIES:	Modern restrooms with showers
PARKING:	Central parking; 5- to 10-minute walk to tent sites
FEE:	$12 for tent sites; $4 per person entrance fee
ELEVATION:	552 feet
RESTRICTIONS:	*Pets:* On leash only *Fires:* In fire rings, but check for burn bans *Alcohol:* Prohibited *Vehicles:* 2 per site *Other:* Maximum 4 persons and one tent per site; guests must leave by 10 p.m.; quiet time 10 p.m.– 6 a.m.; bring your own firewood or charcoal; limited supplies at park store; pick up main supplies in Austin; gathering firewood prohibited

MAP

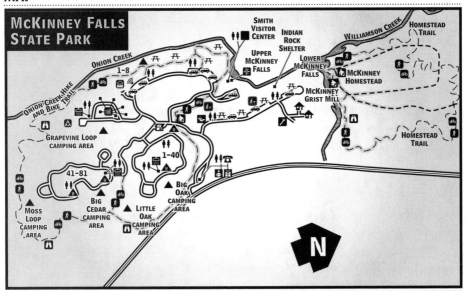

GETTING THERE

From Austin, travel southeast on US 183. Turn right and drive 2.7 miles on McKinney Falls Parkway. Turn right into the park.

GPS COORDINATES

UTM Zone (WGS84)   14R
Easting   623022
Northing   3339487
Latitude   N 30.1806°
Longitude   W 97.7222°

16 MERIDIAN STATE PARK

Don't miss the brillian. lake views in this sought-after destination.

AS YOU ENTER THE TOWN OF MERIDIAN, the peaceful pace of a small town immediately draws you in. The 1886 courthouse sits on the square surrounded by small shops little changed for more than a century. A faded road sign announces you are at the "Top of the Hill Country" and in the home of the "World's Best Barbecue Cook-Off." For Texans, this is a good omen of a special visit.

Leaving town on TX 22, head west and cross the Bosque River. The entrance to Meridian State Park is 2.6 miles on the right. After you turn into the entrance, park headquarters is 0.1 mile ahead. Continue straight ahead for sites 16 through 23 on the right. These sites are sheltered by heavy tree cover and back up to a rocky streambed that would fill up quickly in a typical Texas cloudburst. The sites have good spacing, but get a little road noise from the state highway.

As you continue on the main park road, a low-water crossing and a scenic, hilly, winding road is a reminder of why the Hill Country is such a sought-after destination. The tree cover and thick vegetation come to the edge of the road, with tight turns giving you a glimpse of the lake far below on your right. As you begin your downhill route, watch for a small rock bridge and site 24 shaded by huge cottonwood trees. This solo site is large enough for multiple tents and sits at the edge of a small inlet for the lake. The lake view is excellent and there are no other tents or RVs in sight. You won't have water, electricity, or modern restrooms, but this site is so special that these small inconveniences are no problem.

Leaving site 24, continue for 0.2 miles and watch for an unmarked, paved turnoff on your right. A moderately steep approach will bring you down to a gravel parking lot and lakefront sites 25 and 26. These premier spots have an unobstructed view of the lake, large

RATINGS

Beauty: ✿ ✿ ✿ ✿
Privacy: ✿ ✿ ✿ ✿
Spaciousness: ✿ ✿ ✿ ✿
Quiet: ✿ ✿ ✿ ✿
Security: ✿ ✿ ✿ ✿
Cleanliness: ✿ ✿ ✿

ADDRESS: 173 Park Road 7
Meridian, TX
76665

OPERATED BY: Texas Parks
and Wildlife Dept.

INFORMATION: (254)435-2536

RESERVATIONS: (512)389-8900;
www.tpwd.state
.tx.us

OPEN: All year

SITES: 11 tent-only sites

EACH SITE: 16–23 have water
only; 24–26 have
no water

ASSIGNMENT: Reservations get
you in the camp-
ground; sites are
first come, first
served

REGISTRATION: At headquarters

FACILITIES: Restrooms and
showers near shel-
ters and lake

PARKING: At each site

FEE: Sites 24–26, $13;
sites 16–23, $15;
$5 per person
entrance fee, $3
ages 65 and older,
11 and under free

ELEVATION: 977 feet

RESTRICTIONS: *Pets:* On leash only
Fires: Check with
headquarters for
burn ban
Alcohol: Prohibited
Vehicles: 2 per site
Other: Maximum 8
persons per site;
guests must leave
by 10 p.m.; quiet
time 10 p.m.–
6 a.m.; limited
supplies at head-
quarters; pick up
main supplies in
Meridian; gather-
ing firewood
prohibited

trees, and privacy enough for your entire family or group. The sun sets behind you and you can watch the brilliant colors reflected over the water to the far shore-line. The breeze blows even on the hottest summer eve-nings, and the birds welcome you to their hidden part of the park.

Returning to the main road, turn right for 0.5 miles of steady elevation gain until you reach the Shin-nery Ridge trailhead. This 1.64-mile trail is mostly rough and unspoiled, but the last portion is paved for easy walking and wheelchair access. As you enjoy this area, watch for the usual suspects such as skunks and raccoons, but also try to spot ringtail cats and opos-sums.

Returning on the park road for 1.3 miles, the main park area contains the historic rock structures, picnic areas, and shelters near the swimming cove. Continue 0.2 miles on the one-way road until you reach sites 27 through 29. This grassy area is also lakefront property and shaded by huge trees, but is a little closer to the heavier day-use areas of the park.

As you continue on the park road, the lake is on your left and sheer rock walls are on the right. The Bee Ledge Scenic Lookout is 0.7 miles on your left and is an excellent photography viewpoint for sunsets. As you return to the entrance, watch for roadrunners and white-tailed deer sprinting across the road. As the sun sets, check your rain fly and enjoy the huge thunder-heads building to the east promising the relief of rain and the coming of fall.

RECOMMENDED READING

Walden by Henry David Thoreau, 1854.

VOICES FROM THE CAMPFIRE

"This is a delicious evening, when the whole body is one sense, and imbibes delight through every pore. I go and come with a strange liberty in Nature" (Henry David Thoreau in his essay "Solitude," *Walden*, 1854).

MAP

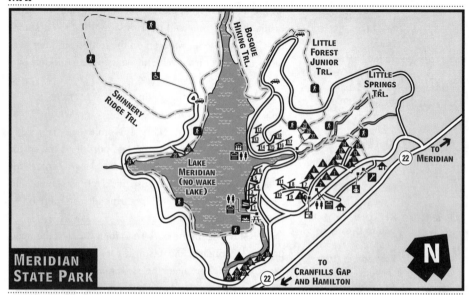

MERIDIAN STATE PARK

Map labels: Bosque Hiking Trl., Little Forest Junior Trl., Little Springs Trl., Shinnery Ridge Trl., Lake Meridian (No Wake Lake), TO Meridian (22), TO Cranfills Gap and Hamilton (22), N

GETTING THERE

From Meridian, go west
on TX 22 for 4 miles.
The park is on the right.

GPS COORDINATES

UTM Zone (WGS84)	14R
Easting	623178
Northing	3529083
Latitude	N 31.8909°
Longitude	W 97.6975°

17
PALMETTO
STATE PARK

> *Premium sites here sit on a peninsula formed by a bend in the wild and scenic San Marcos River.*

SURROUNDED BY EARLY TEXAS HISTORY, Palmetto State Park is 10 miles north of Gonzales, where one of the most famous events on the road to the Alamo occurred, which led to the eventual independence of Texas. On October 2, 1835, just 5 miles southwest of Gonzales on TX 97, the first shot in the Texas Revolution was fired after a group of 18 Texans refused a demand to turn over their only cannon by 150 Mexican dragoons. The Texans' response of "come and take it" has been a part of military history and Texas legend ever since.

After traveling 10.6 miles north from Gonzales on US 183 through rugged ranch land, a left turn onto PR 11 leads to a scenic overlook of the entire valley for perfect sunset pictures. The trees start to close in over the descending road as you approach the village of Ottine. Park headquarters is on your right, and the Warm Springs Hospital Complex looms on the left with a distinct feeling of the 1930s and 1940s.

After leaving the headquarters, continue .2 miles and turn left along Oxbow Lake into the camping area. Shaded by large oaks covered with Spanish moss, sites 20 through 24 back up to a small lake with a playground to the left. Continuing on, sites 38 through 41 surround an artesian well and pond where the local ducks provide the entertainment, along with canoes and paddleboats in season.

Returning to the main road, a right turn takes you deeper into the woods and onto a wide peninsula formed by a bend in the wild and scenic San Marcos River. Sites 25 through 33 are well spaced and back up to heavy brush until you reach the premium sites 34 through 37, which offer river views from a bluff and also enough room to spread out.

After these sites, there is a low water crossing to the group camping area straight ahead, and also a

RATINGS

Beauty: ✪ ✪ ✪
Privacy: ✪ ✪ ✪
Spaciousness: ✪ ✪ ✪ ✪
Quiet: ✪ ✪ ✪ ✪
Security: ✪ ✪ ✪
Cleanliness: ✪ ✪

paved trail to the left that crosses the river to the group pavilion known as the Civilian Conservation Corps (CCC) Refectory. This area is also accessible by car if you return to PR 11, turn left and go 0.5 miles, cross three small bridges, and turn left again.

As you approach the refectory, you pass through backwater areas of palmetto plants, which seem out of place in this part of Texas, but still thrive in this environment of heat, humidity, and heavy spring rainfall. After you park, return to the Palmetto Trail, but do watch for snakes and poison ivy, which are also enjoying this tropical paradise. Be sure to pick up the Palmetto and River Nature trails guidebook at the trailhead. This small pamphlet will enhance your visit and give an excellent description of the wide variety of trees and understory plants here, including Carolina wolfberry, Alabama supplejack, trumpet creeper, and of course, dwarf palmetto. It is worthwhile to make a special stop to see the hydraulic ram pump, which was installed in 1936 to provide CCC workers and park visitors with drinking water. This nonelectric marvel was powered by the artesian well below it and reminds us of the remote and valuable work performed by these hardy workers during the Great Depression.

Upon leaving the trail, return to the parking lot to visit one of Texas's finest CCC buildings. Known as the refectory or "The Concession Building," its original roof was covered with thousands of palmetto leaves and served as the center of CCC camp activity, which included the luxurious provision of regular food, medical, and dental care for the workers. Of particular note, many CCC "boys" actually gained weight, despite their backbreaking labor. As you view this impressive stone structure and its perch overlooking the river, you will come to fully appreciate the CCC workers' contribution to the state of Texas park system and President Roosevelt's vision of the Civilian Conservation Corps.

RECOMMENDED READING

A Journey Through Texas by Frederick Law Olmstead, 1857. (Written prior to the Civil War and prior to Olmstead becoming America's premier landscape architect.)

KEY INFORMATION

ADDRESS:	Route 5, Box 201 Gonzales, TX 78629
OPERATED BY:	Texas Parks and Wildlife Dept.
INFORMATION:	(800) 792-1112 or (830) 672-3266
RESERVATIONS:	(512) 389-8900; www.tpwd.state.tx.us
OPEN:	All year
SITES:	22
EACH SITE:	Picnic table, upright grill, fire ring, lantern hook
ASSIGNMENT:	Reservations get you in the campground; site choice is first come, first served
REGISTRATION:	At headquarters or self-registration station
FACILITIES:	Modern restrooms with showers in RV area, park store
PARKING:	At each site
FEE:	$10 water-only sites; $3 per person entrance fee; under 13 free
ELEVATION:	302 feet
RESTRICTIONS:	*Pets:* On leash only *Fires:* In fire rings *Alcohol:* Prohibited *Vehicles:* 2 per site *Other:* Maximum 8 persons per site; guests must leave by 10 p.m.; quiet time 10 p.m.– 6 a.m.; bring your own firewood or charcoal; limited supplies at park store; pick up main supplies in Gonzales or Luling; gathering firewood prohibited

MAP

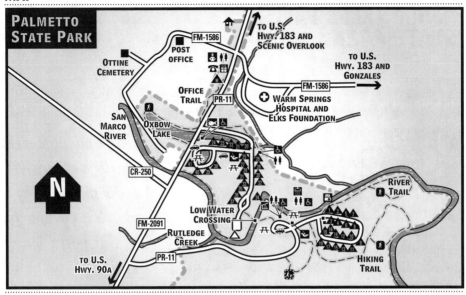

GETTING THERE

From Gonzales, travel 10.6 miles north on US 183. Turn left after 2 miles on PR 11. From Luling, travel 6 miles south on US 183. Turn right on PR 11.

GPS COORDINATES

UTM Zone (WGS84)   14R
Easting   637059
Northing   3274901
Latitude   N 29.5964°
Longitude   W 97.5847°

VOICES FROM THE CAMPFIRE

"The Alamo was one of the earliest of these establishments . . . a mere wreck of its former grandeur . . . The church-door opens on the square, and is meagerly decorated by stucco mouldings, all hacked and battered in the battles it has seen. Since the heroic defense of Travis and his handful of men in '36, it has been a monument, not so much to faith as to courage" (Frederick Law Olmstead, *A Journey Through Texas*, 1857).

18
PEDERNALES FALLS STATE PARK

AS YOU HEAD WEST FROM **AUSTIN** on US 290, you quickly leave the traffic and bright lights of the state's capitol and begin a journey into Texas history. The 38-mile scenic drive brings you to Pedernales State Park, and a sense of remoteness will have you rolling down your car windows and soaking up the smells of the Texas Hill Country.

After leaving the entrance station, an immediate elevation drop brings you closer to the Pedernales River. A right turn at 0.3 miles leads to the parking area for the primitive camping area, an easy 2-mile backpack on Wolf Mountain Trail, which also allows mountain bikers. Continuing on the main road for 0.5 miles, turn right for the main camping area. It has well-spaced campsites that allow both RVs and tents, but the two groups seem to voluntarily separate themselves. The tent campers tend to gather near the nature trail and sites 14 through 31. The sites on the right back up to the river bluff, which is high enough for safety, but close enough to access the river on Trammels Crossing, a short 10-minute walk to the river's edge. The trailhead is next to sites 32 and 34 and descends to the cool, clear waters for wading or shallow swimming. Be sure to bring your water shoes and any other picnic supplies so you can spend the afternoon relaxing on this legendary river.

After you make camp, return to the main road and turn right for 1.4 miles toward Pedernales Falls. From the main parking lot, a leisurely 15-minute walk will bring you to a scenic overlook of the massive rocks smoothed by the river's incredible force during rainy periods. Be sure to read the Flash Flood Warning sign and follow ranger instructions if you plan to walk out into the riverbed. Due to water danger along this unpredictable section of the river, swimming or wading is prohibited.

> *Don't miss the scenic overlook of massive rocks smoothed by the river's incredible force in this Hill Country escape.*

RATINGS

Beauty: ✪ ✪ ✪ ✪
Privacy: ✪ ✪ ✪
Spaciousness: ✪ ✪ ✪
Quiet: ✪ ✪ ✪
Security: ✪ ✪ ✪ ✪
Cleanliness: ✪ ✪ ✪

KEY INFORMATION

ADDRESS:	2585 Park Road 6026 Johnson City, TX 78636
OPERATED BY:	Texas Parks and Wildlife Dept.
INFORMATION:	(800) 792-1112 or (830) 868-7304
RESERVATIONS:	(512)389-8900; www.tpwd.state.tx.us
OPEN:	All year
SITES:	58
EACH SITE:	Picnic tables water, fire ring, lantern hook, electricity
ASSIGNMENT:	Reservations get you in the campground; site choice is first come, first served
REGISTRATION:	At headquarters/entrance station
FACILITIES:	Modern restrooms and shower
PARKING:	At each site
FEE:	$20; $5 per person entrance fee
ELEVATION:	1,029 feet
RESTRICTIONS:	*Pets:* on leash only *Fires:* In fire rings only; check for burn bans *Alcohol:* Prohibited *Vehicles:* 2 per site *Other:* Maximum 8 persons per site; guests must leave by 10 p.m.; quiet time 10 p.m.–6 a.m.; bring your own firewood or charcoal; limited supplies at park store; pick up main supplies in Austin or Johnson City; gathering firewood prohibited

Upon leaving the park, head west on Ranch Road 2766 for 9.3 miles to Johnson City and begin your tour of the Lyndon B. Johnson National Historical Park at LBJ's boyhood home. Travel 14 miles farther west on US 290 and visit the LBJ Ranch, which has been restored to look much as it did when LBJ was the 36th President. Along with his wife, Lady Bird, he entertained national and world leaders on the rocky banks of the Pedernales River.

As you enjoy this tranquil riverside setting, it's easy to see why LBJ used his ranch as a retreat from the stress of politics. It's also easy to imagine the raging Pedernales River and the parallels to LBJ's inner battles to solve the nation's seemingly unsolvable problems. Whatever the mood of the river on your visit, this Hill Country escape is a required stop.

RECOMMENDED READING

Walking it Off: A Veteran's Chronicle of War and Wilderness by Doug Peacock, 2005.

VOICES FROM THE CAMPFIRE

"I wasn't looking for grizzlies but found them anyway. What was invaluable was the way the bears dominated the psychic landscape. After Vietnam, nothing less would anchor the attention. The grizzly instilled enforced humility; you were living with a creature of great beauty married to mystery who could chew your ass off anytime it chose" (Doug Peacock, *Walking it Off: A Veteran's Chronicle of War and Wilderness*, 2005).

MAP

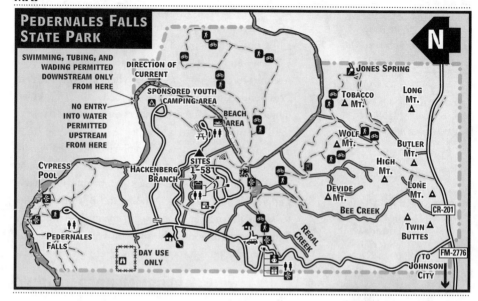

From Austin, drive 32 miles west on US 290, then 6 miles north on FM 3232. From Johnson City, drive 9.3 miles east on Ranch Road 2766.

GPS COORDINATES

UTM Zone (WGS84)	14R
Easting	571391
Northing	3353126
Latitude	N 30.3078°
Longitude	W 98.2575°

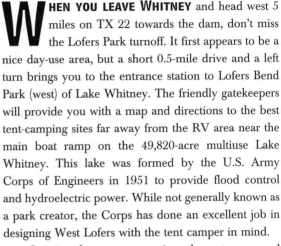

This Corps property is Texas lakeside tent camping at its best.

WHEN YOU LEAVE WHITNEY and head west 5 miles on TX 22 towards the dam, don't miss the Lofers Park turnoff. It first appears to be a nice day-use area, but a short 0.5-mile drive and a left turn brings you to the entrance station to Lofers Bend Park (west) of Lake Whitney. The friendly gatekeepers will provide you with a map and directions to the best tent-camping sites far away from the RV area near the main boat ramp on the 49,820-acre multiuse Lake Whitney. This lake was formed by the U.S. Army Corps of Engineers in 1951 to provide flood control and hydroelectric power. While not generally known as a park creator, the Corps has done an excellent job in designing West Lofers with the tent camper in mind.

Leaving the entrance station, the restrooms and showers are 0.2 miles on your left; a nicely graded rock road is on your immediate right. Turn right and proceed past RV sites 1 through 5 and follow the ridgeline to sites 6 through 10. Sites 8 and 9 are toward the end of the road and provide spectacular lake views. The sites are also very well spaced and allow some real privacy. The oak tree cover provides needed shade in the summer and the lake breezes keep the air temperature pleasant even on the hottest days.

Returning to the main rock road, make a hard right towards the lake and sites 11 through 19. Follow the winding road and arrive at site 14 for an excellent view of the lake and a prepared tent site suitable for two tents. Sites 17 through 19 also have extra room and views of the lake that will have your photographers out at sunrise, sunset, and full-moon rises over the eastern horizon.

Returning on the rock road to the main park road, turn right for 0.1 mile and make an immediate right for sites 20 through 22. Go straight until the road ends at premium site 22, which sits at the tip of the peninsula

RATINGS

Beauty: ✰ ✰ ✰ ✰
Privacy: ✰ ✰ ✰ ✰
Spaciousness: ✰ ✰ ✰ ✰
Quiet: ✰ ✰ ✰
Security: ✰ ✰ ✰ ✰
Cleanliness: ✰ ✰ ✰

with 180-degree views of Lake Whitney and all the people engaged in water sports passing by this elevated overlook. The site is large enough for two or three tents and offers the privacy of truly being at land's end. Remember, you can reserve sites 1 through 46, and site 22 will go fast any time of the year.

Returning to the main road, another immediate right will get you to sites 23 through 27. As with the others, these sites are very well spaced for privacy and solitude. Site 26 will give you huge shade trees and a great view of the lake. Overall, this Corps property is lakeside tent camping at its Texas best!

Leaving tent sites 23 through 27, a right turn will take you to the boat ramp and a very popular RV area. A left turn will return you to the West Lofers entrance station. Be sure to watch for bounding white-tailed deer at any time of day or night as you head straight past the marina turnoff. Of course, the marina does have a park store for emergency supplies such as cold beer. Look for the East Lofers Campground entrance ahead and receive a different map for the 64 individual sites plus 8 sites with a group camp shelter. This is primarily an RV area, but sites 33 through 38 are non-electric sites at lake level that allow you to pull your boat up to the shoreline. There's not much shade, but site 36 puts you out on the waterfront with the sound of waves and wind at your tent's front porch.

RECOMMENDED READING

The Works of Emerson: Four Volumes in One, 1930; *The Harvard Classics: Emerson,* 1909.

VOICES FROM THE CAMPFIRE

"But it is not less that there are books which are of that importance in a man's private experience . . . books which take rank in our life with parents and lovers and passionate experiences" (Ralph Waldo Emerson, 1803–1882, from his essay on books).

KEY INFORMATION

ADDRESS:	100 Lofers Bend Park Road West Whitney, TX 76692
OPERATED BY:	U.S. Army Corps of Engineers
INFORMATION:	(254)694-3189
RESERVATION:	(877) 444-6777; www.recreation.gov
OPEN:	All year
SITES:	64 (East Lofers); 67 (West Lofers)
EACH SITE:	Water, covered picnic table, fire ring, upright grill, lantern hook
ASSIGNMENT:	Reservations available for tent sites; otherwise, first come, first served
REGISTRATION:	At entrance station
FACILITIES:	Modern restrooms with showers
PARKING:	At each site
FEE:	$12 water-only; half price with Golden Age Passport (now known as Senior Pass)
ELEVATION:	557 feet
RESTRICTIONS:	*Pets:* On leash only *Fires:* In fire rings *Alcohol:* Prohibited *Vehicles:* One RV-type vehicle per site; other vehicles not limited *Other:* Maximum 10 persons per site; guests must leave by 10 p.m.; quiet time 10 p.m.–6 a.m.; bring own firewood or charcoal; limited supplies at marina store; pick up main supplies in Whitney or Hillsboro

MAP

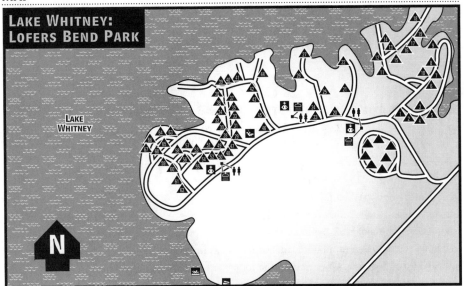

LAKE WHITNEY: LOFERS BEND PARK

LAKE WHITNEY

N

GETTING THERE

From Hillsboro and Interstate 35, travel 18 miles west on TX 22. The park is on right, just before the dam.

GPS COORDINATES

UTM Zone (WGS84)   14R
Easting   654778
Northing   3528269
Latitude   N 31.8797°
Longitude   W 97.3636°

20
LAKE WHITNEY
STATE PARK

WHEN YOU LEAVE **I**NTERSTATE **35** and head west on TX 22 out of Hillsboro, the rolling ranchland does not really prepare you for this lake, with 23,550 surface acres and 70 tent sites to choose from. As you pass the entrance station on the Prairies and Pineywoods Wildlife Trail West, you proceed straight for 0.4 miles until you turn right at the Horseshoe Loop. The tent sites begin at 18, with covered picnic tables on the even-numbered side, which backs up to a heavily wooded area. Continue on the loop road until you see sites 39 through 46, which have nice tree cover and a little extra distance from the RV area.

Return to the main road and proceed 0.5 miles until you see the hiking trailhead on your right. This round-trip walk in the park of 0.9 miles will give you a nice bit of exercise, but do pay attention to the warning signs advising that snakes may be waiting on the trail to welcome you. Of course, when it's 106 degrees on a late July afternoon, the snakes are probably at the lake, which is where you should head next. Proceeding on the main road, the boat ramp is on your immediate right and the swimming area is only 0.3 miles farther. Please note the emphasis on water safety given the rash of drownings at Texas lakes.

Returning to the main road and the beginning of Park Road 47, Whitetail sites 52 through 68 have lake views with covered picnic tables, running water, and some nice trees. Look for site 59, which is not only close to the water but also large enough for your family and sheltered by a massive shade tree.

Turning right for 0.2 miles, you'll come upon Star View sites 69 through 86, which lead you back toward the lake, with sites 76 through 79 nearest the waterfront. Back on the park road, proceed 0.3 miles, where you'll find the new restrooms and showers on your left. At 0.5 miles, the primitive group campground is on the

A great photo-op for sunsets, great blue herons, and even red-headed turkey vultures soaring above.

RATINGS

Beauty: ✿ ✿ ✿ ✿
Privacy: ✿ ✿ ✿
Spaciousness: ✿ ✿ ✿
Quiet: ✿ ✿ ✿
Security: ✿ ✿ ✿ ✿
Cleanliness: ✿ ✿ ✿

ADDRESS:	P.O. Box 1175 Whitney, TX 76692
OPERATED BY:	Texas Parks and Wildlife Dept.
INFORMATION:	(254)694-3793
RESERVATIONS:	(512)389-8900; www.tpwd.state.tx.us
OPEN:	All year
SITES:	70 tent sites
EACH SITE:	Picnic table, central water, fire ring
ASSIGNMENT:	Reservations get you in the campground; site choice is first come, first served
REGISTRATION:	At headquarters
FACILITIES:	Centrally located showers and modern restrooms
PARKING:	At each site
FEE:	$12 water-only sites; $3 per person entrance fee ages 13–65, $2 per person ages 65 and over
ELEVATION:	836 feet
RESTRICTIONS:	*Pets:* On leash only *Fires:* In fire rings *Alcohol:* Prohibited *Vehicles:* 2 per site *Other:* Maximum 8 persons per site; guests must leave by 10 p.m.; quiet time 10 p.m.– 6 a.m.; limited supplies at park store, including firewood; pick up main supplies in Whitney or Hillsboro; gathering firewood prohibited

right. Your eager young campers won't find any shade, but the lake view is super.

The final tent campgrounds are Lakeview/Sunset Ridge sites 111 through 137. The lakefront sites (111 through 123) are made even more attractive by a short rock road directly to the lake's edge and a great photography spot for sunsets, great blue herons, and even a red-headed turkey vulture soaring above. Be sure to continue through Sunset Ridge and take the road that ends at the lake. This wide-open area has a coastal feel, and a private walk on the beach will be a great way to end your tent-camping visit.

As you leave the park, watch for the 2,000-foot airstrip near the deer-crossing sign. If you happen to own a private plane, you can keep your camping gear packed for a quick return to your favorite site and more Lake Whitney beauty.

RECOMMENDED READING

A Sand County Almanac: And Sketches Here and There by Aldo Leopold, 1949.

VOICES FROM THE CAMPFIRE

"Conservation is a state of harmony between men and land. . . . It is inconceivable to me that an ethical relation to the land can exist without love, respect, and admiration for land, and a high regard for its value. By value, I of course mean something far broader than mere economic value; I mean value in the philosophical sense" (Aldo Leopold, *A Sand County Almanac: And Sketches Here and There*, 1949).

MAP

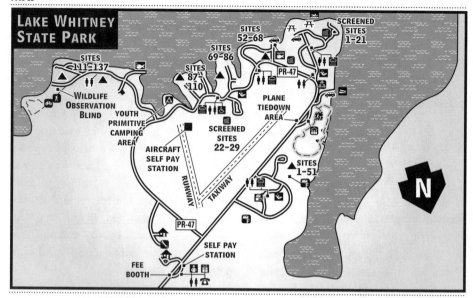

GETTING THERE

From I-35, travel 13 miles
west on TX 22 out of
Hillsboro. Turn right on
FM 1244. The park is
2.4 miles ahead.

GPS COORDINATES

UTM Zone (WGS84)   14R
Easting   655325
Northing   3533977
Latitude   N 31.9311°
Longitude   W 97.3569°

NORTH CENTRAL TEXAS
AND THE LAKE COUNTRY

21

DINOSAUR VALLEY STATE PARK

Glen Rose

LOCATED **LESS THAN TWO HOURS** from the crowded freeways and glass towers of Dallas/Ft. Worth, this weekend getaway is a perfect place to introduce the entire family to tent camping. The park contains 1,523 acres of wide-ranging vegetation (oaks and Ashe junipers in the upland areas and cedar elms in the creek bottoms) across a varied terrain, creating excellent opportunities for day hikes, mountain bike trails, and equestrian areas, and features the real attraction and the park's namesake, a home for dinosaurs. Well, at least dinosaur tracks. These rare and clearly preserved tracks are located mainly at four areas, which are easily accessible depending on the water flow of the clear and cool Paluxy River. The river runs through the park, exposing the tracks in its riverbed. The importance of these sites was recognized by the National Park Service, which designated it as a National Natural Landmark.

First discovered in 1909, the tracks received little attention until 1938, when Roland T. Bird of the American Museum of Natural History visited the site and identified a remarkable double set of tracks left by a giant brontosaurus-like sauropod being followed, maybe pursued, by a large carnivorous dinosaur. While these incredible prints were excavated and hauled off to New York, the park still contains excellent tracks of giant three-toed birds, two-legged carnosaurs, early ancestors of the Tyrannosaurus Rex, and the sauropods, which were 30 to 50 feet long and apparently a tasty meal for the local T-Rex.

Dinosaur Valley State Park was created in 1969 with a small but informative museum attached to the entrance station. Also, there is a gift store located just down the park road with enough dinosaur books, T-shirts, and other gift items to satisfy any parent's

> *A perfect place to introduce the entire family to tent camping.*

RATINGS

Beauty: ☆ ☆ ☆
Privacy: ☆ ☆
Spaciousness: ☆ ☆ ☆ ☆
Quiet: ☆ ☆ ☆
Security: ☆ ☆ ☆ ☆
Cleanliness: ☆ ☆ ☆ ☆

ADDRESS:	Dinosaur Valley State Park P. O. Box 396 Glen Rose, TX 76043
OPERATED BY:	Texas Parks and Wildlife Dept.
INFORMATION:	(254) 897-4588
RESERVATIONS:	(512) 389-8900; www.tpwd.state.tx.us
OPEN:	All year
SITES:	46
EACH SITE:	Picnic table, fireplace, electric hook-up, hanging pole, water tap
ASSIGNMENT:	Reservations get you in the campground; site choice is first come, first served
REGISTRATION:	At entrance station
FACILITIES:	Central bathroom with showers
PARKING:	At sites and trailhead for North Primitive Camping Area
FEE:	$25; $5 per person entrance fee ages 13 and over; ages 12 and under free
ELEVATION:	778 feet
RESTRICTIONS:	*Pets:* On leash only *Fires:* In fireplaces/grates only *Alcohol:* Prohibited *Vehicles:* No limits *Other:* Maximum 8 persons per site; guests must leave by 10 p.m.; quiet time 10 p.m.–6 a.m.; bring your own firewood or charcoal; limited snacks and drinks at gift shop; pick up other supplies in Glen Rose

educational shopping list. If you have trouble finding the gift shop, just look for the two life-size fiberglass models of a 70-foot Brontosaurus and a 45-foot Tyrannosaurus Rex, which were previously seen lurking around the 1964–1965 New York World's Fair. While your first impression may be that these large replicas belong in a Pee Wee Herman movie rather than a state park, they are a magnet for children and give adults a real sense of how monstrous these creatures really were.

Luckily for campers looking for quiet, the campgrounds are located away from the more heavily traveled areas. The first is North Primitive Camping Area, which is accessible only to backpackers willing to make the wet crossing of the Paluxy. The main camping area consists of 46 numbered spots, which have nice tree cover, are well spaced, and contain picnic tables, fireplaces, and a central bathroom/shower facility, but which, unfortunately, also allow RVs and trailers. While this would normally repel the tent camping purist, the arrangement of the spaces with a central area of heavy trees makes it acceptable, especially to the first-time tent camper or a veteran bringing a load of inquisitive young dinosaur hunters.

Given the proximity to a large metropolitan area and its popularity with the fossil mania crowd, the campground can fill up quickly on weekends, so reservations are a must. As with most parks, the earlier you check in, the better your chances to get one of the riverside campsites numbered 13 through 17. These sites are on a bluff backing up to the Paluxy, and normally allow a short hike to the river. Unfortunately, a series of heavy floods have made this access a little more difficult, ending with a 10-foot drop to the riverbed. Don't worry however, as the other river access points are still intact, and a good pair of water shoes will make for easy crossing to the main hiking trails. These trails quickly take on a wilderness feel with nice lookouts over the river and surrounding parklands.

When leaving the park on Park Road 59 (FM 205), don't miss the Fossil Rim Wildlife Park, located to the right on Highway 67. This first-class attraction features a drive-through experience among exotic animals, which are also part of a breeding program for endangered or threatened species, especially cheetahs. The best time to visit is in the morning when the animals are most active.

Turn left on Highway 67 to reach the town of Glen Rose. It offers a number of locally owned restaurants featuring home-style cooking at the MK Corral Restaurant and Saloon, along with barbecue at the Ranch House and Hammonds. Before leaving Glen Rose, travel into the town center to explore a traditional courthouse square surrounded by shops, and note the number of bed-and-breakfast options should the weather turn nasty or the dinosaur ghosts give your kids the spooks. This might happen especially around Halloween, a great time to visit Dinosaur Valley State Park.

RECOMMENDED READING

The Dinosaurs of Dinosaur Valley State Park by James O. Farlow, 1993.

VOICES FROM THE CAMPFIRE

"Every father and mother here, if they are wise, will bring up their children not to shirk difficulties, but to meet them and overcome them, not to strive after a life of ignoble ease, but to strive to do their duty, first to themselves and their families, and then to the whole state" (Theodore Roosevelt, *Strenuous Epigrams,* 1904).

MAP

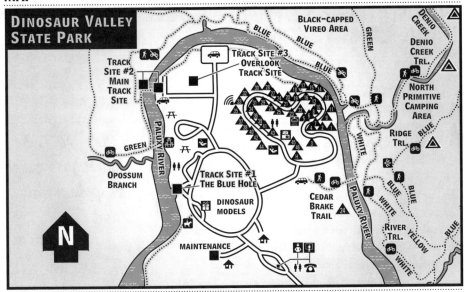

GETTING THERE

From Glen Rose, travel west on Highway 67 to Park Road 59 (FM 205) and turn right. At about 3 miles, stay to the right at the fork. The park entrance is 1 mile straight ahead.

GPS COORDINATES

UTM Zone (WGS84)   14S
Easting   611641
Northing   3568442
Latitude   N 32.2471°
Longitude   W 97.8149°

22
EISENHOWER STATE PARK–LAKE TEXOMA

I**T'S NOT VERY OFTEN THAT TEXANS** and Oklahomans can agree to share anything, but the massive 89,000-acre Lake Texoma that forms a large section of the border between the two states has enough play space for all visitors. The lake was formed in 1944 when the muddy Red River was impounded by the U.S. Army Corps of Engineers. Over the years, the lake has grown so large and deep that except during the wettest season, the lake water is clear and perfect for all forms of boating, from large sailboats and motor yachts to canoes and kayaks. The 580-mile shoreline provides enough hidden coves for some peace and quiet, except for the busiest of holidays in the summer. Just arrive on a weekday and have a local boat guide, a friend familiar with the lake, or a very good lake map. Yes, it really is that big.

After a long day of water sports, the tent camper will enjoy Eisenhower State Park, located on the southern Texas shore near the dam and spillway area. From the entrance station, travel Park Road 20 past the boat ramp, the boathouses, screened-in shelters, and the usual RV sites until you reach Fossil Ridge Campground turnoff at about 1.5 miles. Turn right for tent sites 144 through 165. These sites are heavily treed, and even though the terrain is rocky and hilly, the park has created some nice level tent sites. As you get nearer the water, sites 151 through 154 will give you a little lake view and easy access to a steep but good trail to a small fishing dock. From this dock or from your boat, you can angle for fish of all kinds, including striped bass, slab-sided crappie, and catfish big enough for the tallest tales around the campfire.

Returning to the main road, a short drive of 0.3 miles will take you past the showers/restrooms to Elm Point Camping Area. Follow the signs to sites 167 through 179 and enjoy the views from this peninsula perched high above lake level. Especially in summer,

> *89,000-acre Lake Texoma has enough play space for all visitors.*

RATINGS

Beauty: ✪ ✪ ✪ ✪
Privacy: ✪ ✪ ✪
Spaciousness: ✪ ✪ ✪
Quiet: ✪ ✪ ✪
Security: ✪ ✪ ✪ ✪
Cleanliness: ✪ ✪ ✪

ADDRESS:	50 Park Road 20 Denison, TX 75020-4878
OPERATED BY:	Texas Parks and Wildlife Dept.
INFORMATION:	(903) 465-1956
RESERVATIONS:	(512) 389-8900; www.tpwd.state .tx.us
OPEN:	All year
SITES:	190
EACH SITE:	Tent sites 144–190 have picnic tables, fire rings, water, and lantern hooks
ASSIGNMENT:	Reservations get you in the camp-ground; site choice is first come, first served
REGISTRATION:	At headquarters
FACILITIES:	Restrooms and showers
PARKING:	At each site
FEE:	$14 sites 167–179, other tent sites $12; $3 per person entrance fee ages 13 and over
ELEVATION:	717 feet
RESTRICTIONS:	*Pets:* On leash only *Fires:* In fire rings only *Alcohol:* Prohibited *Vehicles:* 2 per site *Other:* Maximum 8 persons per site; guests must leave by 10 p.m.; quiet time 10 p.m.–6 a.m.; bring your own firewood or charcoal; limited supplies at park store; pick up main supplies in Denison or Sher-man; gathering firewood prohibited

these sites will give you the best breeze while maintaining a nice tree cover of cedar elms and mature oaks. If you arrive early enough and have luck on your side, you can secure Site 179, which offers a 180-degree view of the lake from the rocky point. Just be careful if you sleepwalk or go out for a night stroll. The cliffs are dangerous, and there are no guardrails for the careless or the intoxicated.

Heading back toward the entrance, you can visit the Eisenhower Yacht Club for boat rentals. In Denison, visit the childhood home of President Dwight D. Eisenhower, the park's namesake. Just west of Denison and its neighbor to the south, Sherman, travel west on US Highway 82 to the Hagerman National Wildlife Refuge. This well-known but remote refuge is a popular stopover for migrating birds taking advantage of the Lake Texoma backwaters, ponds, and even cooperating farmers who grow "bird food" crops in the area.

RECOMMENDED READING

Eisenhower: A Centennial Life by Michael R. Beschloss, 1990; *Eisenhower at War* by David Eisenhower, 1986.

VOICES FROM THE CAMPFIRE

"Only those are fit to live who do not fear to die, and none are fit to die who have shrunk from the joy of life and the duty of life. Both life and death are parts of the same Great Adventure" (Theodore Roosevelt, *The Great Adventure,* speaking after the death of his youngest son, Quentin, during World War I).

MAP

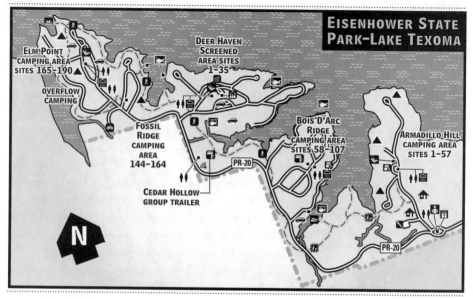

ELM POINT CAMPING AREA SITES 165-190

OVERFLOW CAMPING

DEER HAVEN SCREENED AREA SITES 1-35

FOSSIL RIDGE CAMPING AREA 144-164

CEDAR HOLLOW GROUP TRAILER

BOIS'D'ARC RIDGE CAMPING AREA SITES 58-107

ARMADILLO HILL CAMPING AREA SITES 1-57

PR-20

PR-20

N

GETTING THERE

Take US 75 North from Dallas approximately 75 miles. Go past Sherman, and just north of Denison, exit onto Highway 91. Turn left. Park entrance is 4 miles straight ahead.

GPS COORDINATES

UTM Zone (WGS84)	14S
Easting	722151
Northing	3743713
Latitude	N 33.8103°
Longitude	W 96.6000°

23
LBJ NATIONAL GRASSLANDS

Slow down, open your windows, and keep a sharp watch for a bobcat.

WHEN PLANNING YOUR NEXT tent camping trip, the LBJ National Grassland is a nice surprise. While the name conjures visions of mile after mile of treeless expanse, the area is actually a huge park of trees, lakes, and rolling hills. The trail system covers more than 75 miles, including the 4.1-mile Cottonwood–Black Creek Hiking Trail, which connects the two main tent camping areas.

The initial approach off Highway 287 gives the appearance of modern ranchette civilization, but that quickly gives way after you turn onto CR 2461, 0.5 miles from Black Creek Lake Campground. Be sure to slow down, open your windows, and keep a sharp watch for a bobcat or other animal crossing the road. A sign ahead will direct you to the final 0.5-mile stretch to the Black Creek campground and lake area, which is surrounded by towering pines and oaks. The central parking area contains the self-registration drop, a concrete boat ramp, and the central chemical toilet. The area to your right contains seven campsites allowing drive-in access; these sites also allow RVs without the need for electricity or water hookups.

Most tent campers will head across the wooden bridge where six sites are spread along the water's edge on a slight bluff. The sites are not numbered, but the last one to the left provides the best view of the lake and a trail into the backwoods area, where you will have a good chance to meet white-tail deer, coyotes, and red and gray fox, along with various birds such as quail and wild turkeys. Black Creek does not allow horses or hunting, so your visit should be quiet and rewarding.

Leaving the parking area, return to the main road, turn left for 1.1 miles, and follow the signs to Tadra Point. The road is well-maintained gravel, but watch your speed: the wild turkeys that also use this road

RATINGS

Beauty: ☆ ☆ ☆
Privacy: ☆ ☆
Spaciousness: ☆ ☆ ☆
Quiet: ☆ ☆ ☆
Security: ☆ ☆
Cleanliness: ☆ ☆ ☆

seem rather surprised to hear a vehicle in their territory. In 0.8 miles, turn right at Park Road 900, and turn left into Tadra Point at 0.9 miles. There is a covered pavilion for group events, and the sites provide drive-in convenience along with two modern chemical toilets.

This large campground contains a network of 20 parking spurs and 6 pull-throughs for vehicles with horse trailers. The tree cover is nice, and sites are separated by heavy brush. Some sites sit on a slight downhill slope, but these are also the most remote.

The central road is dirt with gravel and also functions as a horse trail, which is part of a 75-mile trail system for horses, hikers, and mountain bikers. However, be sure to read the informational signs as to which trails allow which use. Also, all horses must have their Coggins certification prior to heading out.

The Tadra Point trailhead functions as the confluence for the trail system. This system is used by local equestrian groups whose volunteer labor created the extensive options into the backcountry. A good sign of remoteness is the bulletin board instructions labeled "what if I get lost."

As a final note, remember to check with the Grasslands headquarters about fire danger and what areas might be open to hunting. Of course, if you are combining tent camping and hunting, then security will probably not be a big concern in this rough backwoods area of North Texas. No matter what activity you enjoy, the rough terrain and the sight of Texans on horseback will be a vivid reminder of the era of cattle drives when nearly 10 million cattle and their escorts traveled north to markets over these vast grasslands.

RECOMMENDED READING

The Texas Rangers: A Century of Frontier Defense by Walter Prescott Webb, 1965. Foreword by Lyndon B. Johnson.

VOICES FROM THE CAMPFIRE

"Had the Indian and not the white man written history, he would have filled it with true stories of the hazardous feats of warriors in carrying their slain or wounded comrades off the field of battle" (Walter Prescott Webb, 1935).

KEY INFORMATION

ADDRESS:	1400 N. Hwy. 81/287 P.O. Box 507 Decatur, Texas 76234
OPERATED BY:	U.S. Forest Service
INFORMATION:	(940) 627-5475
RESERVATIONS:	None
OPEN:	All year
SITES:	40
EACH SITE:	Fire ring
ASSIGNMENT:	First come, first served
REGISTRATION:	Drop box at entrance area to each campground
FACILITIES:	Chemical toilets; no water or electricity
PARKING:	Central parking at Black Creek Lake; parking at sites in Tedra
FEE:	Black Creek, $2 per night or day use; Tadra, $4 per night or day use
ELEVATION:	967 feet
RESTRICTIONS:	*Pets:* On leash only *Fires:* In fire rings only (check for fire danger level) *Alcohol:* Prohibited *Vehicles:* 2 per site *Other:* Maximum 8 persons per site; guests must leave by 10 p.m.; quiet time 10 p.m.– 6 a.m.; bring your own firewood or charcoal; pick up main supplies in Decatur; gathering firewood allowed from downed wood only

MAP

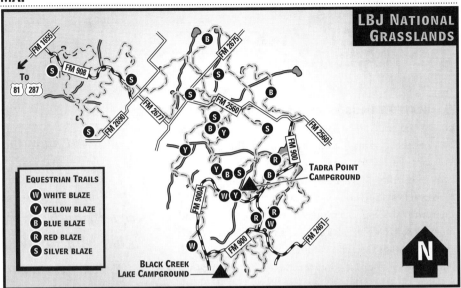

GETTING THERE

From the intersection of US highways 380 and 287 in Decatur, travel 0.5 miles north to the headquarters. Travel 3.3 miles farther north to the rest area turnoff. Make a hard right turn and follow the signs 11.2 miles to Black Creek Lake.

GPS COORDINATES

UTM Zone (WGS84)   14S
Easting   630770
Northing   3690383
Latitude   N 33.3447°
Longitude   W 97.5947°

LOCATED 1 HOUR WEST of Ft. Worth, the gateway to the wide-open spaces of West Texas, this park has the advantage of being at the northern edge of Texas Hill Country, and most importantly, of a 670-acre lake. After leaving the entrance station, the park road reaches an overlook of the lake. A left turn at 0.5 miles will take you to a protected sandy beach area and the park store, which also serves as the rental center for canoes and kayaks. The camping supplies are limited, but the store stocks a good selection of emergency ice cream and cold drinks. Leaving the parking lot, turn left and look for the Lake Mineral Wells Trailway trailhead at 1 mile. This is your connection to more than 22 miles of mountain biking, hiking, and equestrian trails. There is a small charge of $2 for hiking/biking and $4 for equestrian use. Leaving the trailhead parking lot, turn right for a 0.6-mile scenic drive with access to multiple picnic tables high on a bluff overlooking the lake. At the end of the road, park at Penitentiary Hollow and descend the short but narrow trail into the heart of a large boulder field, where local climbers practice their moves. However, don't be fooled by a lack of alpine vistas—a slip of the hand without proper protection can shatter an ankle in a split second.

Returning to the park store/beach area, the spillway turnoff is immediately on your right and serves as the only access to the camping area. The first right at 0.4 miles is for screened shelters 1 through 15 for those campers not ready for tents. The sites run $30 per day and have sufficient space for extra tents. They're situated on a nice bluff overlooking the lake. Back on the main road, turn left at 0.4 miles for the Cross Timbers Camping Area and sites 89 through 108. This water-only area affords some peace and quiet from the electrified RV areas, and it also accesses the 12-mile Cross-Timbers Back Country Trail, which allows hiking, mountain

> *Check out more than 22 miles of mountain biking, hiking, and equestrian trails from Lake Mineral Wells Trailway trailhead.*

RATINGS

Beauty: ✰ ✰ ✰
Privacy: ✰ ✰ ✰
Spaciousness: ✰ ✰ ✰
Quiet: ✰ ✰
Security: ✰ ✰ ✰ ✰
Cleanliness: ✰ ✰ ✰

KEY INFORMATION

ADDRESS: 100 Park Road 71 Mineral Wells, TX 76067

OPERATED BY: Texas Parks and Wildlife Dept.

INFORMATION: (940) 328-1171

RESERVATIONS: (512) 389-8900; www.tpwd.state .tx.us

OPEN: All year

SITES: 108

EACH SITE: Water, picnic table, fire ring, lantern pole

ASSIGNMENT: Reservations get you in the campground; site choice is first come, first served

REGISTRATION: At headquarters

FACILITIES: Showers at all campgrounds except Post Oak; centrally located flush toilets

PARKING: At each site

FEE: $12 per water-only tent site; $5 per person entrance fee, ages 12 and under free

ELEVATION: 539 feet

RESTRICTIONS: *Pets:* On leash only *Fires:* In fire rings or grates only *Alcohol:* Prohibited *Vehicles:* 2 per site *Other:* Maximum 8 persons per site; guests must leave by 10 p.m.; quiet time 10 p.m.– 6 a.m.; bring your own firewood or charcoal; limited supplies at park store; pick up main supplies in Mineral Wells; gathering firewood prohibited

biking, and equestrian use. The central parking lot located at the entrance to the campsite road is also the trailhead for the 2.5-mile Primitive Campground Access Trail for the backpackers in your group looking to pitch their tents away from any motorized, two-wheeled, or four-legged neighbors. Cross-Timbers Campground has showers and bathrooms near site 90, and the heavy tree cover of post oaks, blackjack oaks, and cedar elm provide some privacy and welcome shade.

Returning to the main road, turn left and take an immediate right into Post Oak Camping Area for tent sites 1 through 11. This hilly, rocky, and tree-covered campground runs along the ridge with a lake view. There are no showers, but the small number of sites will give you a more remote feeling, and the lake breeze is a lifesaver in summer.

When leaving the park, be sure to turn right to visit the town of Mineral Wells. This community became famous in the late 1800s when the natural mineral springs became the mecca of tourists seeking the medicinal properties of these healing waters. As you head east back toward Ft. Worth, watch for the sign to Clark Gardens at about 3 miles. This 83-acre botanical garden is a true oasis in this mostly dry West Texas locale and has become an approved test garden for new varieties of roses. It is family-run, and you will likely meet the owners caring for this well-maintained floral paradise. Don't miss the Parker County peaches in Weatherford before returning to the big-city bustle of Ft. Worth.

RECOMMENDED READING

Into Thin Air by Jon Krakauer. (A personal account by the author into the 1996 Mt. Everest disaster.)

VOICES FROM THE CAMPFIRE

"I would never betray a friend to serve a cause. Never reject a friend to help an institution. Great nations may fall in ruin before I would sell a friend to save them" (Edward Abbey, *A Voice Crying in the Wilderness,* 1990).

MAP

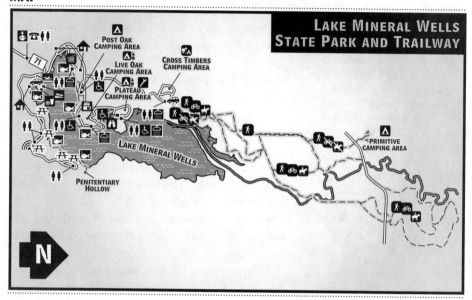

LAKE MINERAL WELLS STATE PARK AND TRAILWAY

Post Oak Camping Area

Live Oak Camping Area

Plateau Camping Area

Cross Timbers Camping Area

Lake Mineral Wells

Penitentiary Hollow

Primitive Camping Area

N

GETTING THERE

From Ft. Worth, travel 20 miles west on I-20, and exit on Highway 180 at Weatherford. Travel 18 miles through Weatherford toward Mineral Wells. Park Road 71 is on your right. Entrance to the park is 2.7 miles straight ahead.

GPS COORDINATES

UTM Zone (WGS84)	14S
Easting	589579
Northing	3630973
Latitude	N 32.8131°
Longitude	W 98.0431°

25
POSSUM KINGDOM
STATE PARK

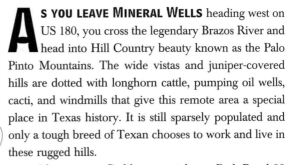

Enjoy beautiful lake views and your own private trail down to the water's edge.

AS YOU LEAVE MINERAL WELLS heading west on US 180, you cross the legendary Brazos River and head into Hill Country beauty known as the Palo Pinto Mountains. The wide vistas and juniper-covered hills are dotted with longhorn cattle, pumping oil wells, cacti, and windmills that give this remote area a special place in Texas history. It is still sparsely populated and only a tough breed of Texan chooses to work and live in these rugged hills.

After passing Caddo, turn right on Park Road 33 and follow the winding paved road for 15 miles until the park entrance sign. Go straight ahead for 0.4 miles and stop at the historical marker on your left that details the hard work of the Civilian Conservation Corps sent here in May 1941 to build the park's infrastructure. As the Second World War began taking in large numbers of recruits, this Corps camp was the last one closed in July 1942. Accustomed to military-type discipline and outdoor experiences, these previously unemployed men were perfect candidates to become the "Greatest Generation."

Continuing past the entrance station for 0.3 miles, turn right on Park Road 33, following the signs toward campsites 22 through 116. 20,000-acre Possum Kingdom Lake appears on your left through the junipers, and the primitive sites are on the left at lake level. These sites are adequate, but probably better as overflow sites. The first numbered sites begin on the left with sites 22 through 25 on the water. Site 26 is the premium waterfront site, where you can hear the waves from your tent. While there is also a huge shade tree with a small, sandy beach, make sure your tent and camping gear are anchored down, since a stiff lake breeze could easily send your lightweight items in for an unplanned swim.

Returning to the main road, turn right at the boat ramp, proceed past the restrooms and showers, and pass

RATINGS

Beauty: ✿ ✿ ✿ ✿
Privacy: ✿ ✿ ✿
Spaciousness: ✿ ✿ ✿
Quiet: ✿ ✿ ✿
Security: ✿ ✿ ✿
Cleanliness: ✿ ✿ ✿

straight through the Shady Grove RV camping area. As you enter the Chaparral camping area, you begin with sites 79 through 81 on the left and a selection of some of the best tent-camp sites in Texas. With covered picnic tables and elevated views of Possum Kingdom Lake, these popular overnight spots fill up quickly.

Proceeding on, the main road splits to the right along interior sites 86 through 99. Beginning with site 100, the lake comes back into view with your own private trail down to the water's edge. Sites 101 through 116 continue along the rocky cliff, providing premier camping with commanding lake views and a wilderness feel. Look for site 113 for the highest point in the campground.

Returning to the main road, turn right toward the park store and marina. Rental boats are available, as well as a protected swimming area and 2.5 miles of hiking trails. Also, don't miss the wide range of birds, including hawks, herons, hummingbirds, and a nice family of turkey vultures more than ready to clean up your tent site should you leave any snacks uncovered. Finally, as you close the tent fly for the night, look for the park's namesake, the opossum. Such a small creature, but in a great park.

RECOMMENDED READING

Goodbye to a River by John Graves, 1960. (A farewell canoe trip down the Brazos River in Texas before it was dammed and changed forever.)

VOICES FROM THE CAMPFIRE

"In that place the stark pleasures of aloneness and unchangingness and what a river meant did not somehow seem to be very explicable. . . . You are not in a hurry there; you learned long since not to be" (John Graves, *Goodbye to a River,* 1960).

KEY INFORMATION

ADDRESS:	P.O. Box 70 Caddo, TX 76429
OPERATED BY:	Texas Parks and Wildlife Dept.
INFORMATION:	(940) 549-1803
RESERVATIONS:	(512) 399-9900; www.tpwd.state .tx.us
OPEN:	All year
SITES:	17 at Lakeview; 37 at Chaparral Trail
EACH SITE:	Picnic table, fire ring, upright grate
ASSIGNMENT:	Reservations get you in the campground; site choice is first come, first served
REGISTRATION:	At headquarters
FACILITIES:	Modern restrooms and showers, park store, canoe and kayak rentals
PARKING:	At each site
FEE:	$7 primitive, $12 water-only; $4 entrance fee, under 13 free, over 65 $2, over 78 free
ELEVATION:	1,033 feet
RESTRICTIONS:	*Pets:* On leash only *Fires:* In fire rings or grates only *Alcohol:* Prohibited *Vehicles:* 2 per site *Other:* Maximum 8 persons per site; guests must leave by 10 p.m.; quiet time 10 p.m.– 6 a.m.; bring your own firewood or charcoal; limited supplies at park store; pick up main supplies in Mineral Wells or Breckenridge; gathering firewood prohibited

MAP

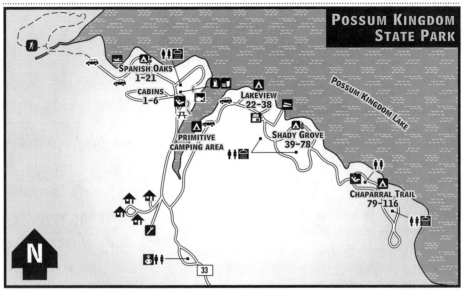

GETTING THERE

Drive 35.5 miles west of
Mineral Wells on US 180,
then 17 miles north on
Park Road 33.

GPS COORDINATES

UTM Zone (WGS84)   14S
Easting   541010
Northing   3637714
Latitude   N 32.8768°
Longitude   W 98.5616°

26
PURTIS CREEK STATE PARK

LOCATED ALONG HIGHWAY 175 and near the gateway to heavily treed East Texas, Purtis Creek State Park is a prime fishing lake. The 355-acre lake was designed and built to control floodwaters but has become a first-class destination for anglers who don't want to fight the speedboat crowd. There is a 50-boat limit on the lake, and the no-wake rule is strictly enforced, with a speed limit appropriately described as "idle."

Turning north off Highway 175, you'll approach the park past tranquil farms and small ranches. After leaving the headquarters, you'll see the lake almost immediately, with sites 60 through 64 straight ahead near the boat docks and protected swimming area. These sites are perfect for families out for a weekend of water fun, but those looking for solitude should proceed to the primitive campground parking lot and take the short nature trail to sites A through M. After leaving your car, follow the easy dirt trail across two small wooden bridges and then to a fork. The left fork takes you to the chemical toilet. The right fork crosses the third wooden bridge. About 5 minutes later, you'll arrive at a nicely constructed bird-watcher's blind complete with an opening for cameras or binoculars. The trail continues along the edge of this very quiet backwater area until you reach sites A through M in about another 5 minutes. These nicely spaced sites are primitive, but they have the advantage of privacy and waterfront views for the more than 200 bird species that call this park home at different times of the year. However, the most unique feature is the ability to pull your boat up to a smooth landing and deliver your camping gear by boat rather than pack it in by the trail. The park even rents canoes by the hour or the day.

This area was also home to Native Americans who left petroglyphs just east of the park, indicating this land was also good for hunting. As the frontier was

> *Sample the pleasures of fishing, bird-watching, and quiet boating while enjoying the shade of massive oaks and junipers in this family-friendly park.*

RATINGS

Beauty: ✿ ✿ ✿
Privacy: ✿ ✿ ✿
Spaciousness: ✿ ✿ ✿
Quiet: ✿ ✿ ✿ ✿
Security: ✿ ✿ ✿ ✿
Cleanliness: ✿ ✿ ✿

KEY INFORMATION

ADDRESS:	14225 FM 316 Eustace, TX 75124
OPERATED BY:	Texas Parks and Wildlife Dept.
INFORMATION:	(903) 425-2332
RESERVATIONS:	(512) 389-8900; www.tpwd.state .tx.us
OPEN:	All year
SITES:	18
EACH SITE:	Sites A–M, fire rings; sites 60–64, water taps; picnic tables and bathrooms nearby
ASSIGNMENT:	Reservations get you in the campground; site choice is first come, first served
REGISTRATION:	At headquarters
FACILITIES:	Bathrooms and showers at multiuse camping area
PARKING:	Small paved lot near trailhead
FEE:	$6 primitive sites (A–M), $10 wateronly sites (60–64); $2 per person entrance fee
ELEVATION:	374 feet
RESTRICTIONS:	*Pets:* On leash only *Fires:* In fire rings only; firewood is $3 per stack at host site 16 *Alcohol:* Prohibited *Vehicles:* 2 per site *Other:* Maximum 8 persons per site; guests must leave by 10 p.m.; quiet time 10 p.m.– 6 a.m.; bring your own firewood or charcoal; limited supplies in Eustace; main supplies in Kaufman or Athens

explored and conquered, the conflict between Native Americans and white settlers flared and resulted in the death of famed Cherokee Indian Chief Boles, who was slain in the battle of Neches in 1839 near the town of Edom.

For the tent camper today, it is easy to see the attraction for all those who have passed here before. The abundant wildlife, rich vegetation, and clean water were vital to survival then and provide a perfect escape from the clogged freeways of the big city today. While the bass fishing is world-class, don't miss the many canoeing activities, including classes in basic canoe skills and even a Full Moon Canoe Tour. Canoes and kayaks are available for rental and provide the serenity and relaxation only calm water can supply. Whatever your interest, don't miss this hidden gem a little more than an hour from Dallas.

RECOMMENDED READING

60 Hikes within 60 Miles Dallas/Fort Worth by Joanie Sanchez, 2008.

VOICES FROM THE CAMPFIRE

"On the one hand, we thrive on the diverse cultural, entertainment, and dining offerings of our cosmopolitan city; on the other hand, we long for the open prairies, wooded creeks, and wildflower fields that the freeways, shopping centers, and gas stations have replaced" (Joanie Sanchez, *60 Hikes within 60 Miles Dallas/Fort Worth,* 2008).

MAP

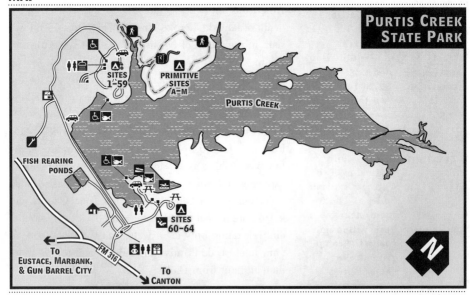

GETTING THERE

From Highway 175 between
Kaufman and Athens, travel
north on FM 316 for
3.3 miles to the park
entrance on the left.

GPS COORDINATES

UTM Zone (WGS84)	14S
Easting	782033
Northing	3584723
Latitude	N 32.3639°
Longitude	W 96.0028°

27
RAY ROBERTS STATE PARK: ISLE DU BOIS UNIT AND JOHNSON BRANCH

As an urban escape, anytime is a great time to visit.

THERE IS SOMETHING ATTRACTIVE about large bodies of water, especially when they are less than 1.5 hours from the urban sprawl of Dallas–Ft. Worth. Located just north of the college town of Denton, Lake Ray Roberts is a 30,000-surface-acre reservoir with an irregular shoreline, which creates numerous peninsulas, backwater coves, and a sense of wildness not found in many man-made bodies of water. The large expanses of water serve as perfect sunrise and sunset reflectors as well as a summer playground for the power-boat set, which tells you that the best times to tent-camp here are during the week or anytime from late September to early May. Of course, this also corresponds with the best time to tent-camp in north Texas since daytime summer temperatures here are often over 100°F and nighttime temperatures may not drop below 80°F. However, the presence of the lake will also give you a refreshing breeze, a place to rent canoes, and a protected swimming area near the park store. Given this park's proximity as an urban escape, anytime is a great time to visit.

Turning north off FM 455, the headquarters and entrance station of the Isle du Bois unit is 0.4 miles ahead. After paying your fees and picking up the park map, proceed past the small interpretive center and travel 1.5 miles to the Hawthorn Camping Area and turn left. The large paved parking lot and modern restrooms may not look like the access point to a wilderness tent-camping experience, but the best is hidden from immediate view. On your left, near the restrooms, are paved trails that lead to sites 6, 7, and 17, which are perfect for wheelchair access or other campers not able to walk to the wooded areas immediately behind these close-in sites.

As you proceed on the paved trail, it quickly gives way to a mostly gravel pathway, which is suitable for

RATINGS

Beauty: ✿ ✿ ✿
Privacy: ✿ ✿ ✿ ✿
Spaciousness: ✿ ✿ ✿ ✿
Quiet: ✿ ✿ ✿
Security: ✿ ✿ ✿ ✿
Cleanliness: ✿ ✿ ✿ ✿

easy hiking or even the use of carts (available for rent at the camp store) to transport your camping gear to sites 8 through 15. As you walk, the stands of oak and elm become thicker and the sites get further apart. By the time you see the water, sites 10, 11, 13, 14, and 15 will give you waterfront views and the parking lot will not be visible, even though the walk will have been less than 15 minutes.

If these sites are full or don't suit your desires, return to the parking lot and proceed to the end where a similar set of close-in sites (18 through 21) would probably be acceptable, if you are not camping on a crowded weekend. However, continue into the woods and follow the trail until it splits at the directional sign. Sites 22 through 28 are to the right, but the better choice is to the left, where sites 29 through 34 will give you the camping experience of a more remote park. Those sites follow the shoreline and are spaced to give you privacy and solitude. Sites 34A and 34B are especially nice for families who want the kids close, but not too close. Sites 27 and 29 are group sites that give excellent views of the lake, but are the farthest from the parking lot at about 20 minutes. The more you are able or willing to walk, the more secluded the sites; these walks would even make for a good beginner backpack experience.

Leaving the Hawthorn Camping Area, turn left and travel for 0.7 miles until you see the Wild Plum Area parking lot on your left. Take the paved bicycle path for about 50 yards until you see the Wild Plum sign. The chemical toilets and campsites begin in about 75 yards. These sites (117 through 130) are in a nice grove of oak trees and are very close to a backwater cove; however, they also overlook the very large paved boat ramp area. While some park visitors would find it desirable to be near this very busy spot in the summer, the tent camper looking for some peace and quiet should return to Hawthorn, hike a little extra distance, and listen to the abundant bird life—including songbirds like cardinals and soaring red-tailed hawks being chased by local grackles.

After leaving Isle du Bois, return to Interstate 35 North, take Exit 483, and travel 7 miles east on FM 3002

KEY INFORMATION

ADDRESS: 100 PW 4137 Pilot Point, TX 76258

OPERATED BY: Texas Parks and Wildlife Dept.

INFORMATION: (940) 686-2148

RESERVATIONS: (512) 389-8900; www.tpwd.state .tx.us

OPEN: All year

SITES: 55 (Isle du Bois); 154 (Johnson Branch)

EACH SITE: Picnic table, fire ring with grate

ASSIGNMENT: Reservations get you in the campground; site choice is first come, first served

REGISTRATION: At headquarters

FACILITIES: Restroom at Hawthorn Area lot; chemical toilet at Wild Plum Area; showers at ramp and RV areas

PARKING: Central paved lot for tent sites

FEE: $12 tent sites; $5 per person entrance fee

ELEVATION: 651 feet

RESTRICTIONS: *Pets:* On leash only *Fires:* Check with headquarters; stoves OK *Alcohol:* Prohibited *Vehicles:* 2 per site *Other:* Maximum 8 persons per site; guests must leave by 10 p.m.; quiet time 10 p.m.– 6 a.m.; bring your own firewood or charcoal; limited supplies at park store; pick up main supplies in Sanger or Denton

to the north shore of 30,000-acre Lake Ray Roberts, where the Johnson Branch provides the tent camper two totally different experiences. Just 0.4 miles after the entrance station, turn right into the Dogwood Canyon central parking area. From this location, you can unload your mountain bike and test your skills on nearly 9 miles of trails rated for different levels of expertise and used by the Dallas Off-Road Bicycle Association (**www.dorba.org**).

After a hard day on the bike, return to the parking lot and follow the dirt trail toward the lake and campsites 135 through 154. Look for sites 149 and 150 with waterfront access and views on a quiet backwater slough suitable for canoes, kayaks, or a little fishing. The area is heavily wooded and the sites are spaced for privacy.

If you are looking for more of a lake experience, return to the park road, turn right and go past the RV campgrounds for 1.5 miles and arrive at Oak Point. This large area contains the park store, picnic areas, boat ramps, modern restrooms and showers, and a 180-degree view of the lake. The central parking for tent sites 106 through 134 is on your right, and a short walk will give you a great view and all the cool lake breezes you need. On busy weekends, there are also three overflow campgrounds with 25 additional sites. Look for nine sites in overflow area C. These sites are right on the water and have covered picnic tables as well as a view of all the lake action, including windsurfers and parasailing.

If you are bringing the family or need a place to float in peace, there is also a wide sandy beach with a protected swimming area. It is located behind the restrooms and overflow campsite A. Just follow the campers, hikers, bikers, and swimmers as they tow their ice chests to this popular area. The park store has limited supplies, but does have rental boats to explore this large lake, which is located only 1.5 hours from Dallas or Ft. Worth.

RECOMMENDED READING

"The Pond in Winter" chapter in *Walden* by Henry David Thoreau.

VOICES FROM THE CAMPFIRE

"I shall look from the same window on the pure sea-green Walden water there, reflecting the clouds and the trees, and sending up its evaporations in solitude, and no traces will appear that a man has ever stood there" (Henry David Thoreau, *Walden*, 1854).

MAP

RAY ROBERTS STATE PARK:
ISLE DU BOIS UNIT AND JOHNSON BRANCH

To PILOT POINT & 377

JORDAN PARK

BLUESTEM GROVE 171-184

HAWTHORN 1-40

FM 455

DEER RIDGE 41-116

QUAIL RUN 132-170

WILD PLUM 117-131

To SANGER & 35

N

RAY ROBERTS LAKE

GETTING THERE

ISLE DU BOIS

From I-35, north of Denton, exit at Sanger. Take FM 455 east about 10 miles to the park entrance. From Pilot Point and US 377, take FM 455 West to the entrance.

JOHNSON BRANCH

Take I-35 North from Dallas or Ft. Worth. Go past Denton and take Exit 483. Go east on FM 3002 for 7 miles. Park entrance is on the right.

GPS COORDINATES

UTM Zone (WGS84)   14S
Easting   680692
Northing   3700581
Latitude   N 33.4294°
Longitude   W 97.0564°

SOUTH TEXAS AND
THE GULF COAST

WHEN YOU ARE READY TO ESCAPE the crowded confines of the big city, this special park will take you deep into our early history as Texans and even further—a lot further. The area was not only a part of the original Stephen F. Austin land grant in the 1820s but also an earlier home to the Karankawa Indians, whose reported cannibalistic habits now only seem fitting for the park's most popular current resident, the American alligator. Throw in a specific warning for venomous snakes and you have a chance to observe wild animals in their habitat, not yours.

This special park will take you deep into our early history as Texans and even further.

As you leave US 59 and turn onto FM 762, you soon pass the outer limits of suburbia and the George Ranch Historical Park on your right. Follow FM 762 for 11.4 miles, then enter the park on Park Road 72. The headquarters is straight ahead and surrounded by massive live oaks covered with Spanish moss. On a clear, sunny day, you sense this camping and hiking experience will have some significant rewards. On a foggy, rainy day, you will feel as if the prehistoric world of dinosaurs awaits you.

At 0.3 miles, you'll spot a large picnic area on your left, overlooking the 40-acre lake. Be sure to check out the multiple nature programs offered at this popular park, such as photo walks, bird-watching events, and of course, the Gatorwise Club for those young tent campers looking to satisfy their curiosity about these prehistoric descendants. Continuing on the main road, the huge trees begin to close over the pavement to form a canopy of shade. You begin to notice the lowlands on both sides of the road for 2.5 miles until you reach the large parking lot at the nature center, where hands-on exhibits attract the kids, and helpful volunteers suggest the best 'gator viewing areas.

Across the street are two must-see sites. The first is the George Observatory, with three domed telescopes

RATINGS

Beauty: ✪ ✪ ✪ ✪
Privacy: ✪ ✪ ✪
Spaciousness: ✪ ✪ ✪
Quiet: ✪ ✪ ✪
Security: ✪ ✪ ✪ ✪
Cleanliness: ✪ ✪ ✪

KEY INFORMATION

ADDRESS: 21901 FM 762
Needville, TX
77461

OPERATED BY: Texas Parks
and Wildlife Dept.

INFORMATION: (979) 553-5101;
www.brazosbend
.org

RESERVATIONS: (512) 389-8900;
www.tpwd.state
.tx.us

OPEN: All year

SITES: 73; 13 shelters

EACH SITE: Picnic table, fire
ring, water,
electricity,
lantern hook

ASSIGNMENT: Reservations get
you in the camp-
ground; site
choice is first
come, first served

REGISTRATION: At headquarters

FACILITIES: Restrooms with
showers, observa-
tory, gift shop,
museum, youth
group primitive
camping area

PARKING: At each site

FEE: $20; shelters $25;
$3–$5 entrance fee

ELEVATION: 74 feet

RESTRICTIONS: *Pets:* On leash only
Fires: In fire rings
Alcohol: Prohibited
Vehicles: 2 per site
Other: Maximum 8
persons per site;
guests must leave
by 10 p.m.; quiet
time 10 p.m.–
6 a.m.; bring your
own firewood or
charcoal; limited
supplies at park
headquarters and
gift store; pick up
main supplies in
Richmond, Sugar-
land, or Houston

and public viewing on Saturdays from 3 to 10 p.m. Call (979) 553-3400 for details. The other is the 0.5-mile Creekfield Interpretive Trail, which circles Creekfield Lake for some close-up views of the local waterfowl. With the park's proximity to the Texas coast and its status as part of the Brazos River floodplain, the chance to see more than 300 species makes this a bird-watcher's and photographer's gold mine.

Returning to the main road, turn right to the Burr Oak Camping Area and sites 100 through 141. These large sites have electricity and a fair number of RVs. Fortunately, they are spacious, with sites 120 through 123 and 106 and 107 located on the ends for a little extra privacy to spread out into the woods.

Leaving Burr Oak, stay to the right for the Red Buckeye Camping Area sites 200 through 234. This area also has electrified RVs, but sites 215 through 217 and 232 through 234 give the best chance for some solitude. In late 2009, be sure to ask about a tent-only area being considered in the meadow behind sites 230 and 232.

As you complete the Red Buckeye Circle, screened shelter sites 1 through 13 offer a good alternative to the RV areas. Pitch your tent outside the shelter and use it for a mosquito escape or severe storm shelter if necessary.

Returning to the main road, turn right toward Elm Lake and a chance to see some wetland areas that truly qualify as wild lands. Following the 1.7-mile Elm Lake Loop Trail, you immediately see large areas of disturbed mud and brush along the shoreline. It looks as if a truck or tractor went off the elevated pathway, but you soon learn these are the unmistakable signs of the American alligator. Of particular interest on the day I hiked was a very large 10- to 11-foot 'gator happily sunning himself on a small island just 40 or 50 feet from the hikers quickly snapping pictures and holding onto their small children. After seeing this massive animal enjoying a midday nap, you understand the necessity for "Alligator Etiquette" and keeping your dogs on a short leash away from the water.

While the alligators (and all the others) move throughout the park, you have 22 miles of hiking and mountain-bike trails to enjoy this premier destination

MAP

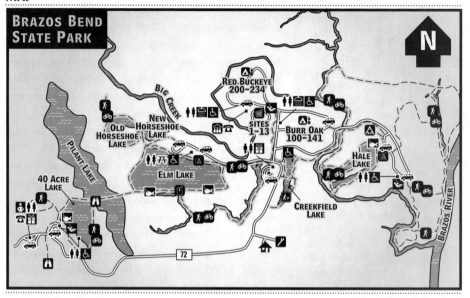

just a little over an hour from the Houston skyline and its own cement jungle. So when you need a break, come here for a taste of the real jungle. You won't be disappointed.

RECOMMENDED READING

A Birder's Guide to the Texas Coast by Harold R. Holt, 1993.

VOICES FROM THE CAMPFIRE

"It is not enough to understand the natural world; the point is to defend and preserve it" (Edward Abbey, 1989).

GETTING THERE

From Houston, travel southwest on US 59. Exit onto FM 762 near Richmond. Turn left and follow FM 762 for 18 miles to the park entrance on your left.

GPS COORDINATES

UTM Zone (WGS84)	15R
Easting	244575
Northing	3251946
Latitude	N 29.3708°
Longitude	W 95.6314°

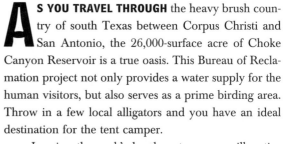

> *With names like Owl Hollow, Hawk Alley, and Dove Place, you know to bring your binoculars, spotting scopes, and long-range camera lenses.*

A S YOU TRAVEL THROUGH the heavy brush country of south Texas between Corpus Christi and San Antonio, the 26,000-surface acre of Choke Canyon Reservoir is a true oasis. This Bureau of Reclamation project not only provides a water supply for the human visitors, but also serves as a prime birding area. Throw in a few local alligators and you have an ideal destination for the tent camper.

Leaving the park's headquarters, you will notice deer-crossing signs, very healthy cacti, mesquite grasslands, and widespread Tamaulipan thorn shrubs. Turn right at the T-intersection toward the camping areas and tent sites 200 through 215. The 75-acre lake is on the immediate right; sites 206 through 215 have clear views of this small lake and the numerous birds enjoying its protected shores. Don't be fooled though by its calmness; a quick look at the shore vegetation reveals a good deal of disturbance by the local alligators. The tent sites are elevated from the shoreline, but do follow the park instructions for "alligator etiquette."

Continue on the circle to sites 200 through 205 for premium waterfront sites on the main reservoir. You get all the benefits of the lake breeze here, plus sunrise views over a large portion of the lake without an RV in sight.

As you return on the main road, a number of bird-watching trails have been cleared from the dense vegetation. With names like Owl Hollow, Hawk Alley, and Dove Place, you know to bring your binoculars, spotting scopes, and long-range camera lenses. In addition to permanent residents such as the long-billed and curve-billed thrashers, look for Audubon's Orioles and brown-crested and vermillion flycatchers, along with nearly 300 other species listed in the field checklist available at the park headquarters.

Continuing on the main road, turn left into the shelter area for tent-camping sites 1 through 20. Look

RATINGS

Beauty: ✿ ✿ ✿
Privacy: ✿ ✿
Spaciousness: ✿ ✿ ✿
Quiet: ✿ ✿ ✿ ✿
Security: ✿ ✿ ✿
Cleanliness: ✿ ✿ ✿

for sites 12 through 20 for great waterfront and sunset views. This area would be especially attractive if your group contains non-tent campers or the weather turns unexpectedly dangerous. Just reserve a shelter and put your tent up next door in the surrounding grassy area. You get the great water view and the RVs are down the road out of sight.

After locating your tent site, grab your hiking partner and head into the heavy bush. Birds are literally all around as you explore over 12,500 acres in this wildlife management area. When you return to the picnic area, keep an eye out for cave swallows who nest under the roofs of shelters. While many of the bird species pass through at various times of the year, the park is most popular in winter when the warm South Texas weather attracts bird enthusiasts from all over the world. However, be aware that a sudden cold snap can arrive without much warning, so pack your heavy sleeping bag just in case. During late spring, summer, and early fall, the heat and humidity can be a real danger to day hikers who walk too far from their tent without sufficient water, a wide-brimmed hat, or sunscreen.

As you leave the park and turn left for 7.3 miles, be sure to visit the South Shore Unit and the area below the dam. This riparian woodland area is home to shorebirds, herons, egrets, and even passerines. It also follows the Frio River, which was dammed to create Choke Canyon Reservoir and provide abundant fishing opportunities in the 75-acre lake stocked with bass, bluegill, white crappie, and channel catfish.

RECOMMENDED READING

The Birds of Texas by John L. Tveten, 1993.

VOICES FROM THE CAMPFIRE

"We need wilderness because we are wild animals. Every man needs a place where he can go to go crazy in peace. Every Boy Scout Troop deserves a forest to get lost, miserable, and starving in" (Edward Abbey, *The Journey Home,* 1977).

KEY INFORMATION

ADDRESS:	PO Box 2 Calliham, TX 78007
OPERATED BY:	Texas Parks and Wildlife Dept.
INFORMATION:	(361) 786-3868
RESERVATIONS:	None
OPEN:	All year
SITES:	16 tent-only sites; 20 shelter sites
EACH SITE:	Picnic table, fire ring, lantern hook
ASSIGNMENT:	Reservations get you in the campground; site choice is first come, first served
REGISTRATION:	At headquarters
FACILITIES:	Modern restrooms and showers; boat ramp; fishing pier; sponsored youth-group area
PARKING:	Near each site
FEE:	$12 walk-in waterfront sites; $3 entrance fee ages 13 and over, those under 13 free
ELEVATION:	196 feet
RESTRICTIONS:	*Pets:* On leash only *Fires:* In fire rings with grates; check on burn bans *Alcohol:* Prohibited *Vehicles:* 2 per site *Other:* Maximum 8 persons per site; guests must leave by 10 p.m.; quiet time 10 p.m.–6 a.m.; bring your own firewood or charcoal; limited supplies at Three Rivers; pick up main supplies in San Antonio or Corpus Christi; gathering firewood prohibited

MAP

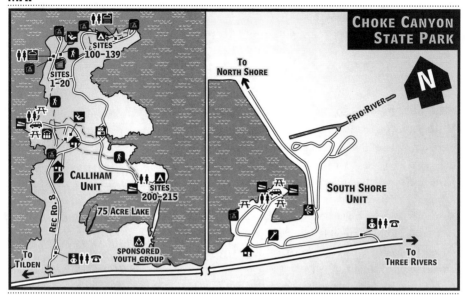

GETTING THERE

From I-37 exit onto TX 72
and turn west. Follow the
signs in Three Rivers and
pass South Shore Day-Use
Area. Continue on to North
RR 8. Park headquarters is
1.3 miles ahead.

GPS COORDINATES

UTM Zone (WGS84)   14R
Easting   563222
Northing   3149006
Latitude   N 28.4661°
Longitude   W 98.3542°

30
GOOSE ISLAND
STATE PARK

DON'T BE FOOLED BY THE SIZE of this 314-acre park. Goose Island State Park sits in the middle of some of the most important and beautiful natural areas of Texas. Whether you are coming from the northeast through miles and miles of the 59,000-acre Aransas National Wildlife Refuge or from the southwest and the white beaches of Corpus Christi, always be alert for some incredible wildlife. Even an old abandoned farmstead on TX 35 can yield the view of lifetime. I spotted a pair of whooping cranes (a critically endangered species) near sunset here, less than 75 yards from the roadside during the peak winter bird-watching season. These magnificent five-foot-tall birds—along with 300 other recorded species—make this portion of the Texas coast a bird-watcher's gold mine.

For the tent camper, an immediate right after the entrance station into the wooded area brings you to sites 201 through 203. This area of dense trees provides a welcome bit of shade in this expanse of open coastal vegetation. Continuing on the Lantana Loop, tent sites 207 through 209 are close to the road, with sites 210 through 218 back in the woods for extra privacy. If these sites are full, consider sites 151 and 152, which have electricity but are divided by heavy-enough brush to shield your tent from any nearby RVs. When you pass site 157, also look for the 0.66-mile Turks Cap Trail for a close-up view of local bird life.

Once you set up camp, the real adventure begins. Serious birdwatchers, photographers, and fisherman should return to the main road and turn right toward the Bay Front Area and the Recreation Hall Area, with its tall palm trees and resort feel. This is the meeting point for many of the guided nature tours that may come upon some of the 11 whooping cranes who resided in the park during 2009. There are also ample fishing opportunities for speckled trout, redfish, drum,

300 recorded species, including the magnificent whooping crane, make this portion of the Texas coast a bird-watcher's gold mine.

RATINGS

Beauty: ✮ ✮ ✮ ✮
Privacy: ✮ ✮ ✮
Spaciousness: ✮ ✮ ✮
Quiet: ✮ ✮ ✮
Security: ✮ ✮ ✮
Cleanliness: ✮ ✮ ✮

ADDRESS:	HC04 Box 105 Rockport, TX 78382
OPERATED BY:	Texas Parks and Wildlife Dept.
INFORMATION:	(800) 792-1112, (361) 729-2858
RESERVATIONS:	(512) 389-8900; www.tpwd.state.tx.us
OPEN:	All year
SITES:	225
EACH SITE:	Picnic table, fire rings/grates, central water, lantern hooks
ASSIGNMENT:	Reservations get you in the campground; site choice is first come, first served
REGISTRATION:	At headquarters
FACILITIES:	Boat ramp, fishing pier, restrooms with showers
PARKING:	Near each site
FEE:	$10 per night; $3 per person entrance fee ages 13 and over
ELEVATION:	26 feet below sea level
RESTRICTIONS:	*Pets:* On leash only *Fires:* In fire rings *Alcohol:* Prohibited *Vehicles:* 2 per site *Other:* Maximum 8 persons per site; guests must leave by 10 p.m.; quiet time 10 p.m.– 6 a.m.; bring your own firewood or charcoal; limited supplies at park store; pick up main supplies in Rockport or Corpus Christi; gathering firewood prohibited

flounder, and sheepshead, should you wish to bring home your own dinner for the campfire. Photographers should follow the road across the small bridge for Bayfront sites 1 through 45. While these sites attract RVs like a mosquito on a summer night, the sunset view across the bay toward Corpus Christi is perfect for that low-light exposure. Be sure you have a tripod if the herons agree to pose in a perfect spot just off the bank.

Returning to park headquarters, travel straight on Park Road 13 north toward The Big Tree. This state champion coastal live oak is estimated to be more than 1,000 years old, have a circumference of 35 feet, and a crown of 90 feet. It is also close to Fourth Street Pond, where the black-crowned night herons roost, joined by an occasional yellow-crowned night heron and especially abundant warblers. Whatever your reason for visiting, put down your tent and stay a few days in this wildlife bonanza.

Before you leave this area, you must visit the Aransas National Wildlife Refuge. Return to TX 35 and turn right onto FM 774E. Proceed 9 miles and take another right onto FM 2040E. The entrance gate to Aransas National Wildlife Refuge is 6.5 miles straight ahead. This world-famous refuge has the largest number of whooping cranes in North America. The cranes' seven-foot wingspan and distinctive bugle call make them the centerpiece of intense efforts to save the entire ecosystem. A 16-mile auto tour features numerous exhibits and viewing areas. Of course, if you don't care to bird-watch, the alligator viewing area is always a treat for the whole family. Don't miss it.

RECOMMENDED READING

Return of the Whooping Crane by Robin W. Doughty, 1989.

VOICES FROM THE CAMPFIRE

"The sight of a Whooping Crane in the air is an experience packed with beauty and drama. We see the broad sweep of the great wings in their stiff, almost ponderous motion, the flash of sunlight on the satin white plumage" (Robert P. Allen, *The Whooping Crane*, 1952).

MAP

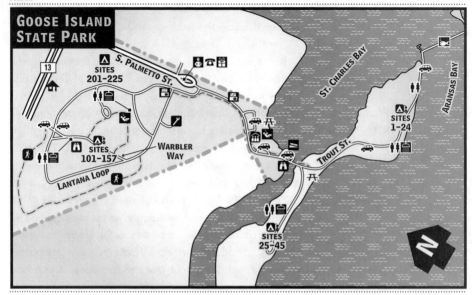

GETTING THERE

From Rockport, travel 12 miles northeast on TX 35. Turn right onto Park Road 13 for 1.7 miles to the entrance station.

GPS COORDINATES

UTM Zone (WGS84)	14R
Easting	697977
Northing	3113589
Latitude	N 28.1331°
Longitude	W 96.9842°

> *The simple act of walking for miles on the white-sand beaches will bring you back every year.*

ONLY **20** MILES FROM DOWNTOWN Corpus Christi, follow the Cross-town Expressway over the JFK Causeway to TX 361 north. Turn left and drive for 5 miles, leaving the hotels, condos, and civilization behind. The entrance to Mustang Island State Park is on the right, and upon entering the park, the Gulf of Mexico is straight ahead.

Named after the herds of wild mustangs that roamed this area until the late 1800s, this premier tent-camping area is located on the beach. As you approach the sand dunes, the RV sites are to the left in a parking lot where you cannot see the beach or the ocean, but where you'll find showers and restrooms. Continuing on, turn right toward Beach Camping and the crashing waves become your constant companion, along with sea gulls overhead. Using the beach as your roadway, look for a prime spot to pitch your tent. The unmarked campsites are along the dunes so you can pick a tent location as far away from your neighbor as possible. Remember that the dunes are part of a fragile ecosystem and the only real protection for the island, so don't stray off the beach. There are also snakes in the dunes in case you need another reason to stay off.

After securely staking down your tent and putting up the rain fly in case of a squall line off the gulf, begin winding down from whatever stress you had in the city. There are more than 400 bird species that either live on the island or pass through during migratory season, so a pair of binoculars or a good telephoto lens will add to your experience. You might also enjoy some extended beachcombing. Periodic storms and crashing waves constantly bring in new shells along with food for a wide range of shorebirds, including the quick plovers, killdeers, and sandpipers darting beside the stately herons, long-billed curlews, and ponderous pelicans. The fishing is also excellent from the jetty or the shore, but

RATINGS

Beauty: ✿ ✿ ✿ ✿
Privacy: ✿ ✿ ✿
Spaciousness: ✿ ✿ ✿ ✿
Quiet: ✿ ✿ ✿ ✿
Security: ✿ ✿ ✿
Cleanliness: ✿ ✿ ✿

the real enjoyment here lies in the therapeutic waves and the almost-constant sea breeze. When you add the unlimited views to the horizon, the simple act of walking for miles on the white-sand beaches will bring you back every year, even if that lightning-fast sea gull stole your lunch when you weren't looking.

Recent storms have washed up some extra debris, so remember to pack up your trash so the seabirds don't mistake it for food. There can also be a strong undertow not too far off the shoreline, along with a stinging jellyfish or two. Whatever your activity, a little extra caution will make this seaside beauty a tent camper's real paradise.

Heading inland, notice the intricate set of dunes that also protect the island from the occasional hurricane. These deep-rooted coastal grasses and vines are essential to preventing beach erosion by both wind and storm surge. They also protect the area's small mammals such as pocket gophers, ground squirrels, mice, and cotton rats. These important inhabitants are key food sources for the soaring hawks as well as coyotes and bobcats. While these animals may be hard to find during the day, their tracks will be a reminder that barrier islands are an ecosystem worth protecting.

RECOMMENDED READING

Silent Spring by Rachel Carson, 1962.

VOICES FROM THE CAMPFIRE

"I contend, furthermore, that we have allowed these chemicals to be used with little or no advance investigation of their effect on soil, water, wildlife, and man himself. Future generations are unlikely to condone our lack of prudent concern for the integrity of the natural world that supports all life" (Rachel Carson, *The Obligation to Endure,* 1962).

KEY INFORMATION

ADDRESS:	P. O. Box 326 Port Aransas, TX 78373
OPERATED BY:	Texas Parks and Wildlife Department
INFORMATION:	(361) 749-5246
RESERVATIONS:	(512) 389-8900; www.tpwd.state.tx.us
OPEN:	All year
SITES:	Unlimited on the beach
EACH SITE:	Central water, portable toilets, rinsing showers nearby
ASSIGNMENT:	Reservations get you in the campground; site choice is first come, first served
REGISTRATION:	At entrance station
FACILITIES:	Modern restrooms and showers
PARKING:	At each site
FEE:	$8 beach camping; $4 per person entrance fee, ages 12 and under free
ELEVATION:	6 feet
RESTRICTIONS:	*Pets:* On leash only *Fires:* In fire rings only *Alcohol:* Prohibited *Vehicles:* 2 per site *Other:* Maximum 8 persons per site; guests must leave by 10 p.m.; quiet time 10 p.m.– 6 a.m.; bring your own firewood or charcoal; limited supplies at park store; pick up main supplies in Corpus Christi; gathering firewood prohibited

MAP

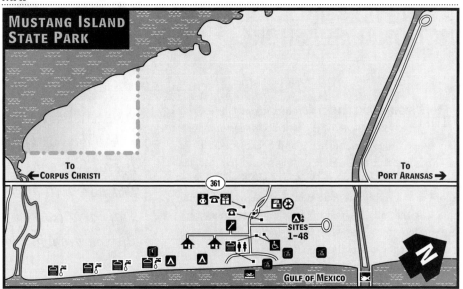

GETTING THERE

From Corpus Christi, cross the JFK Causeway. Travel north on TX 361. The park entrance is 5 miles ahead on the right.

GPS COORDINATES

UTM Zone (WGS84)   14R
Easting   680055
Northing   3062224
Latitude   N 27.6722°
Longitude   W 97.1744°

A S YOU LEAVE THE CITY of Corpus Christi, the wide-open spaces of the world's longest undeveloped stretch of barrier island beckons you like a siren's song. For those tent campers who live too far inland, a yearly journey to Padre Island National Seashore is an essential requirement for renewing the soul in a way that only a great body of untamed water can. As you look over the waves to an endless horizon, you instantly begin to feel the big city leave you, and a primal connection to the earth return.

Approaching the park entrance on Park Road 22, miles and miles of grass-covered sand dunes flank the way. There are no buildings in sight and even the old cattle fences have been removed. Depending on the latest storm, the roadway may still have blown sand along the way, which only adds to the anticipation. Prior to the entrance station, the North Beach Access Road to your left allows camping and is also a popular day-use area. Passing into the national seashore, you'll see a nature trail at 0.2 miles on your right and the Bird Island Basin turn-off in 0.7 miles. Continue on for 2.5 miles and turn left onto 20410 Park Road, heading for the Malaquite Beach Campground. This is primarily an RV campground, but there are six tent-only sites at either end of the parking lot, along with restrooms and showers. The beach is somewhat hidden by the dunes, but the picnic tables on the beach are closer to the water.

Leaving Malaquite, the visitor center is only 1 mile away, but the change in feeling is distinct. While the parking lot is large, the center itself is built into the landscape with classic "parkitecture," such that you have a sense of approaching a frontier outpost, not a government building. The rustic decking and skin-saving shade structures house the small museum, a park store, and modern restrooms with excellent showers. There are also elevated platforms for not only ocean views but

> *A few days at Padre Island National Seashore will help shake whatever big-city ills you brought along.*

RATINGS

Beauty: ✪ ✪ ✪ ✪
Privacy: ✪ ✪ ✪
Spaciousness: ✪ ✪ ✪ ✪ ✪
(on the beach)
Quiet: ✪ ✪ ✪ ✪
(on the beach)
Security: ✪ ✪ ✪
Cleanliness: ✪ ✪ ✪ ✪

ADDRESS: P. O. Box 181300 Corpus Christi, TX 78480

OPERATED BY: National Park Service

INFORMATION: (361) 949-8068; (361) 949-8173; www.nps.gov/pais

RESERVATIONS: None accepted

OPEN: All year

SITES: 6 tent sites in Malaquite; approx. 10 unmarked sites at Bird Island Basin; unlimited sites on beach

EACH SITE: Malaquite: picnic table with shelter; Bird Island Basin: picnic table with shelter, grill

ASSIGNMENT: First come, first served

REGISTRATION: At visitor center or self-reg. kiosks

FACILITIES: Visitor center, park store, restrooms with showers

PARKING: At each site

FEE: $8 (Malaquite); $5 (Bird Island Basin); no charge (beach); $10 per vehicle entrance fee

ELEVATION: 11 feet

RESTRICTIONS: *Pets:* On leash only *Fires:* In fire rings *Alcohol:* Prohibited *Vehicles:* 2 per site *Other:* Maximum 8 persons per site; guests must leave by 10 p.m.; quiet time 10 p.m.– 6 a.m.; bring your own firewood or charcoal; limited supplies at visitor center; pick up main supplies in Corpus Christi

also your first look far down the beach and sand dunes where you see . . . more beach and sand dunes. Even from the visitor center, you begin to realize this is the start of a very large stretch of wilderness where everyone can spread out and have the type of space modern society has so often taken away.

Leaving the parking lot, the paved road curves between the sand dunes, and the white sands become your new highway. The self-registration station is on your immediate right, where you pick up your free Back Country Use Permit. Proceeding on the beach, which is considered a public highway in Texas, you drive on the firm sand near the crashing waves, but not too near. In choosing a site, you have the first 5 miles to pick the amount of space desired between you and any other campers. There are periodic portable toilets, which may also impact your choice.

If you have a four-wheel drive, you can extend your wilderness camping range another 60 miles or so, but keep in mind the sand is very unpredictable and even a four-wheel drive may get stuck. Regardless of where you choose, a tent pad in the soft sand is a true outdoor luxury. Add the constant sound of the waves, the calling seabirds, and the cooling breeze, and you have a premier tent-camping experience. Just be sure to stake down your tent and put up your rain fly, because those beautiful towering clouds way out on the Gulf might be coming your way in the middle of the night. If they do, it will still be a great camping experience to hold your tent walls with both arms outstretched and then tell all your friends how you survived the raging storm from the high seas while your fellow car camper jumped in the backseat of the vehicle.

Returning to the visitor center for a necessary shower, keep a close watch for the often-hidden Kemp's Ridley sea turtle nests or even the highly endangered turtles themselves, or their offspring 'racing' for the water and freedom. From June to August, Padre Island National Seashore is home to these amazing creatures, whose popularity has caused more than 3,000 people to attend releases of the incubated hatchlings back to the sea.

Head back toward the front-entrance gate, and the turn-off for Bird Island Basin is on your left. This campground and day-use area is the new hot spot in the park, where windsurfing on the usually placid Laguna Madre attracts surfers from all over the country. Rentals and lessons are available along with tent camping at the far end of the RV/camper sites. The tent sites are unnumbered, but there are ten parking spots set aside for tent campers.

Whether you are racing across the Laguna Madre or walking on the beach alongside sea birds racing the tides, a few days at Padre Island National Seashore will help shake whatever big-city ills you showed up with.

RECOMMENDED READING

Healing the West: Voices of Culture and Habitat by Jack Loeffler, 2008.

VOICES FROM THE CAMPFIRE

"Because all organisms have descended from a common ancestor, it is correct to say that the biosphere as a whole began to think when humanity was born. If the rest of life is the body, we are the mind. Thus, our place in nature, viewed from an ethical perspective, is to think about the creation and to protect the living planet" (Edward O. Wilson, *The Future of Life,* as quoted by Jack Loeffler in *Healing the West: Voices of Culture and Habitat,* 2008).

MAP

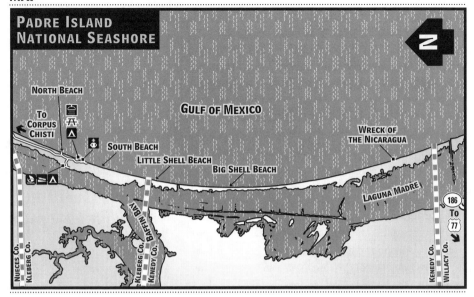

GETTING THERE

From Corpus Christi, take TX 358 to South Padre Island Drive and cross the JFK Causeway to Park Road 22. Turn right onto Park Road 22; the entrance station is approximately 10 miles ahead.

GPS COORDINATES

UTM Zone (WGS84)   14R
Easting   668180
Northing   3034626
Latitude   N 27.4247°
Longitude   W 97.2986°

LOCATED BETWEEN HOUSTON and Victoria off US 59, this campground seems remote for human travelers, but is situated perfectly for migratory birds heading to and from the Texas coast. As you enter the park, you are protected by heavy tree cover. Once you take an immediate left across the bridge, wildlife appears near the road, including the armor-plated armadillo and the majestic great blue heron searching for food in a backwater cove starved for rain by the recent years of drought. You also see the Texana trailhead, which connects to approximately 4.5 miles of hiking trails that are perfect for wildlife photography and solitude.

Hiking trails leading from the Texana trailhead are perfect for wildlife photography and solitude.

Continuing straight on the main road you'll see non-electric sites 1 through 26, arranged on both sides of the road for easy access, but also some RV traffic passing through to the multiuse camping area. After site 26, make a hard right for much-larger sites 27 and 29, which back up to the cove for premier waterfront views. Continue on to site 31 for not only water views, but also an end location shaded by a huge tree. While all 14 lakeside sites are very good, choose 39 and 42 for easiest access to the lighted fishing pier; move farther away for privacy and darkness. The interior sites are also well spaced, with heavy brush shielding many of them from the neighboring tents.

Returning to the main road, continue across the second bridge into the RV area and multiple sites on the main Lake Texana. Turn right toward the nature center for canoe and kayak rentals. These normally peaceful modes of transportation may come with a little extra adventure given the presence of a few American alligators basking under the watchful gaze of red-headed turkey vultures. These massive but elegantly sleek birds sit in dead trees observing the tourists picnicking on the water's edge. The birds patiently wait for the humans to

RATINGS

Beauty: ☆ ☆ ☆
Privacy: ☆ ☆ ☆
Spaciousness: ☆ ☆ ☆
Quiet: ☆ ☆ ☆ ☆
Security: ☆ ☆ ☆ ☆
Cleanliness: ☆ ☆ ☆ ☆

KEY INFORMATION

ADDRESS:	P. O. Box 760 Edna, Texas 77957
OPERATED BY:	Texas Parks and Wildlife Department
INFORMATION:	(361) 782-5718
RESERVATIONS:	(512) 389-8900; www.tpwd.state.tx.us
OPEN:	All year
SITES:	55
EACH SITE:	Picnic table, fire ring and grate, lantern hook, central water
ASSIGNMENT:	Reservations get you in the campground; site choice is first come, first served
REGISTRATION:	At headquarters
FACILITIES:	Modern restrooms and showers; lighted fishing pier
PARKING:	At each site
FEE:	$10 per night; $3 entrance fee ages 13 and over, $2 ages 65 and over
ELEVATION:	20 feet
RESTRICTIONS:	*Pets:* On leash only *Fires:* In fire rings *Alcohol:* Prohibited *Vehicles:* 2 per site *Other:* Maximum 8 persons per site; guests must leave by 10 p.m.; quiet time 10 p.m.–6 a.m.; bring your own firewood or charcoal; limited supplies at park store; pick up main supplies in Victoria or Ganado; gathering firewood prohibited

depart, then swoop silently down for an evening meal of any food carelessly left behind.

Returning to your campsite, be sure to get to bed early. Sunrises over the lake are the perfect backdrop for photographing the white-tailed deer and the abundant bird life preparing to head back north as spring approaches. These birds include more than 225 species spending part of their winter in the park and the Matagorda Bay area just to the south. The birds then migrate along a narrow bottleneck on the great Central Flyway, which links North America with Central and South America. Depending on the time of year, look for shorebirds, waterfowl, gulls, terns, raptors, passerines, and maybe even a flock of Baird's sandpipers on their nonstop flight to or from the high Arctic.

While watching the birds, you can also fish for largemouth bass, crappie, and catfish along the 125 miles of shoreline. Of course, don't be too distracted to notice the signs of an American alligator. If you see disturbed mud and crushed shoreline brush that looks like a vehicle got stuck in it, just move to another spot and continue enjoying your stay at this lesser-known but very interesting park.

RECOMMENDED READING

Walden: 150th Anniversary Illustrated Edition of the American Classic by Henry David Thoreau, 2004 (photographs by Scot Miller).

VOICES FROM THE CAMPFIRE

"Most men, even in this comparatively free country, through mere ignorance and mistake, are so occupied with the factitious cares and superfluously coarse labors of life that its finer fruits cannot be plucked by them . . . Most of the luxuries, and many of the so-called comforts of life, are not only not indispensable, but positive hindrances to the elevation of mankind" (Henry David Thoreau, *Walden,* 1817–1862).

MAP

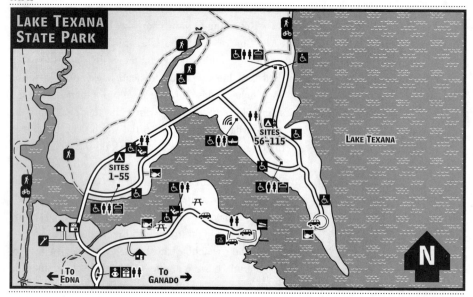

From Houston take US 59
south and turn left on
TX 172 in Ganado. Turn
right on TX 111. Cross the
lake and turn right into
the park entrance.

GPS COORDINATES

UTM Zone (WGS84)		14R
Easting		739094
Northing		3205446
Latitude	N	28.9547°
Longitude	W	96.5467°

THE TEXAS PANHANDLE, HIGH
PLAINS, AND CAPROCK CANYONS

34 LAKE ARROWHEAD STATE PARK

LOCATED LESS THAN **30 MINUTES** from the city of Wichita Falls, this 16,200-acre lake attracts not only fishing enthusiasts from all over north Texas and southern Oklahoma, but also serves as a retreat for Midwestern College students and Sheppard's Air Force Base personnel. Especially in the summer, the lake breeze and swimming area are essential to surviving the hot weather made famous by the Hotter than Hell 100 bicycle race. There is also a 5.5-mile hike-horse-bike trail for those trying to get a little exercise.

As you leave the entrance station, there is a disc golf course built into a grove of heavy mesquite, which adds to the game's challenge. There is also a modern equestrian campground with four sites that include electricity.

Returning to the main road, the lake appears on the horizon, where sometimes campers will see a red-tailed hawk racing low over the trees looking for lunch. Continue past the day-use area on the right until the road turns toward the lake and sites 61 through 67. These spacious level sites are within view of the lake and near the prairie dog town, which is active with these cute—but definitely wild—cousins of the squirrel. The prairie dogs move quickly between mounds, but always seem to be wary of hawks or other predators on the hunt. The campsites are also close to the fishing pier and swimming area at the road's end.

Back on the main road, turn right just past site 61 to reach sites 57 through 60, which are arranged around a circular drive. These well-spaced sites are away from the traffic and have some tree cover. Look for site 59 with its large grass-covered tent pad and a view over the backwater areas of the lake. Bring your camera and binoculars to scan this area for bird activity in the early morning or late afternoon. Turning right out of the circle, sites 49 through 56 also line the backwater area,

> *Bring your camera and binoculars to scan this area for bird activity.*

RATINGS

Beauty: ☆ ☆ ☆
Privacy: ☆ ☆ ☆
Spaciousness: ☆ ☆ ☆
Quiet: ☆ ☆ ☆
Security: ☆ ☆ ☆ ☆
Cleanliness: ☆ ☆ ☆

ADDRESS:	Route 2, Box 260 Wichita Falls, TX 76310
OPERATED BY:	Texas Parks and Wildlife Dept.
INFORMATION:	(940) 528-2211
RESERVATIONS:	(512) 389-8900; www.tpwd.state .tx.us
OPEN:	All year
SITES:	18
EACH SITE:	Covered picnic table, fire ring, water
ASSIGNMENT:	Reservations get you in the campground; site choice is first come, first served
REGISTRATION:	At headquarters
FACILITIES:	Restrooms in picnic area, restrooms and showers in RV area, boat ramp, swimming area
PARKING:	At each site
FEE:	$10 per night water-only sites; $2 per person entrance fee; ages 12 and under free
ELEVATION:	942 feet
RESTRICTIONS:	*Pets:* On leash only *Fires:* In fire rings *Alcohol:* Prohibited *Vehicles:* 2 per site *Other:* Maximum 8 persons per site; guests must leave by 10 p.m.; quiet time 10 p.m.– 6 a.m.; bring your own firewood or charcoal; limited supplies at headquarters; pick up main supplies in Wichita Falls; gathering firewood prohibited

but are a little closer together. They are also the tent sites nearest to the modern restrooms and showers in the RV area.

As you leave the park, note the Primitive Group Camping Area Trail for those beginning backpackers and campers preparing for their next trip to wilder parts of Texas or beyond. This 5.5-mile trail allows hikers, mountain bikers, and equestrians. It is moderately strenuous, so be sure to bring sufficient water. Whether you are trying out new hiking boots, a new backpack, or just trying to get in shape, this trail is a good fit.

After you hit the trail, return to your campsite, grab your fishing gear or swimsuit, and head for the lake. There is a large protected swimming area just across the grassy area from tent sites 61 through 67, and next to it is the fishing pier and fish-cleaning station for those crappie, catfish, bass, and perch. The water-skiing crowd will appreciate the nice boat ramp in summer.

Given this lake's location near the edge of the arid West Texas frontier, fill your water bottles, get a big hat and a strong walking stick, and make your reservations early.

RECOMMENDED READING

The New Complete Walker by Colin Fletcher, 1974 and later editions.

VOICES FROM THE CAMPFIRE

"Most of my wandering in the desert I've done alone . . . I generally prefer to go into places where no one else wants to go. I find that in contemplating the natural world my pleasure is greater if there are not too many others contemplating it with me, at the same time. However, there are special hazards in traveling alone. Your chances of dying, in case of sickness or accident, are much improved" (Edward Abbey, *Desert Solitaire,* 1968).

MAP

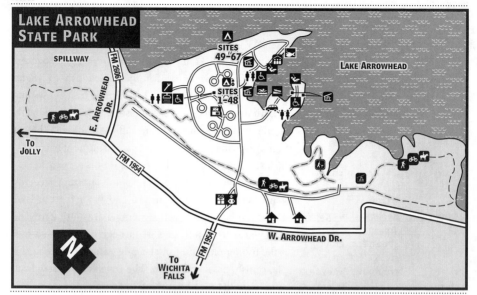

GETTING THERE

Travel 8 miles south of Wichita Falls. Turn left on FM 1954. The park entrance is 7.6 miles straight ahead.

GPS COORDINATES

UTM Zone (WGS84)	14S
Easting	556056
Northing	3735522
Latitude	N 33.7583°
Longitude	W 98.3947°

35
CAPROCK
CANYONS
STATE PARK

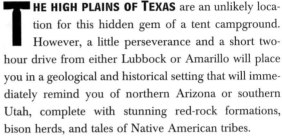

> *"Caprock Canyons State Park will immediately remind you of northern Arizona or southern Utah.*"

THE HIGH PLAINS OF TEXAS are an unlikely location for this hidden gem of a tent campground. However, a little perseverance and a short two-hour drive from either Lubbock or Amarillo will place you in a geological and historical setting that will immediately remind you of northern Arizona or southern Utah, complete with stunning red-rock formations, bison herds, and tales of Native American tribes.

As you travel across the panhandle, covering miles of tabletop-flat cotton fields, the sudden change of encountering the Caprock escarpment with its rugged hills and valleys is a welcome sight. The small town of Quitaque (pronounced kitty-quay) is renovating its old main street buildings with the hope that visitors to this relatively new state park and its unique trail system will bring to the area a necessary revival.

Leaving the main road (TX 86) and traveling north on FM 1065 for 3.5 miles, you will arrive at the new visitor center to pay your fees and enjoy a fine overlook of Texas bison. Mary Ann and Charles Goodnight, who recognized that the bison were quickly becoming extinct, started this herd on the famous JA Ranch, which is now Caprock Canyons. By 1929, the herd increased in number to around 250 and was used to help re-populate Yellowstone National Park. The herd now runs freely through a large section of the park and is a powerful symbol of this region of Texas and of how Native Americans lived in harmony with the land before their conflict with western expansion led to decades of war, relocation, and near extermination of the bison.

Proceeding past the visitor center 0.5 miles, you arrive at Lake Theo and tent-camping sites 1 through 10. Look for the small gravel parking lot and a nice wide trail of about 100 yards that leads to the lakeside sites. Site 1 on the far left is on an elevated peninsula, which will provide a little extra air flow in the summer.

RATINGS

Beauty: ☆ ☆ ☆ ☆
Privacy: ☆ ☆ ☆
Spaciousness: ☆ ☆ ☆
Quiet: ☆ ☆ ☆ ☆
Security: ☆ ☆ ☆ ☆
Cleanliness: ☆ ☆ ☆ ☆

The other sites are adequate, but the surrounding ground is not very level for pitching a tent. Unless you have to have waterfront property, the other campsites will probably interest you more.

In the next 0.3 miles, the Honey Flat Campground turnoff leads you and the RV crowd to their allotted spaces and the only shower facilities in the park. These showers are more than adequate and this campground effectively keeps the larger vehicles away from the wilder areas of the park. Returning to the main park road, you begin to see the scale of red-rock beauty in this little-known park. This view of the canyon escarpment resembles a smaller version of the Vermillion Cliffs near the North Rim of the Grand Canyon and leads to the unique Wildhorse Campground, which allows you to bring horses along with your RV or trailer. While not a tent-camping area, the presence of horses and designated horse trails here echoes 19th-century cattle drives and the true Texas heritage of a cowboy surviving on the range many miles from home.

As you leave Wildhorse, the road drops at a 16-percent grade and begins a journey into the park, which will reward tent campers for their efforts. In 1.6 miles, turn into Little Red Tent Camping Area and park in the central parking lot. Tent sites 56 through 65 surround the lot and can be reached easily. Each site has a flat tent area along with a covered picnic table, fire pit, and grill. The rustic composting toilets next to site 61 are clean and more than adequate. The sites all have excellent views over the canyon area, with site 65 perched perfectly overlooking the Little Red River. When staying at this small campsite, you forget the RVs and asphalt you left behind. As sunset approaches, you enjoy the sound of wind through the canyons and the pace of life slows to meet your own desires.

The final two stops are the North Prong Primitive Camping Area and the South Prong Tent Camping Area. The first requires a 1-mile backpacking hike, and the second contains tent sites numbered 36 through 55, which have no covered tables and fire pits only. While these sites lack the seclusion of Little Red, they all share a 360-degree view of the red-rock formations and are close to the Upper Canyon Trail.

KEY INFORMATION

ADDRESS:	PO Box 204 Quitaque, TX 79255
OPERATED BY:	Texas Parks and Wildlife Dept.
INFORMATION:	(806) 455-1492
RESERVATIONS:	(512) 389-8900; www.tpwd.state.tx.us
OPEN:	All year
SITES:	40
EACH SITE:	Amenities vary
ASSIGNMENT:	Reservations get you in the campground; site choice is first come, first served
REGISTRATION:	At entrance station
FACILITIES:	Restrooms and showers at RV area; restroom at Lake Theo; compost toilets at South Prong and Little Red areas
PARKING:	Central parking
FEE:	$14 (Lake Theo); $12 (South Prong and Little Red); $3 per person entrance fee
ELEVATION:	2,569 feet
RESTRICTIONS:	*Pets:* On leash only *Fires:* Charcoal only in fire pits and grills; call ahead to check on fire danger level *Alcohol:* Prohibited *Other:* Maximum 8 persons per site; guests must leave by 10 p.m.; quiet time 10 p.m.–6 a.m.; bring your own charcoal; no supplies at entrance station; limited supplies in Quitaque or Turkey

As in all areas of the park, be sure to remember you are in west Texas; while the local deer are cute and the bison magnificent, other wildlife includes a few rattlesnakes, which may not take kindly to you wandering off the trail.

As a final part of your visit, be sure to check out the Caprock Canyons Trailway, which crisscrosses the area for an incredible 64 miles. This trail system was created from abandoned railroad right-of-ways and features a 742-foot tunnel, complete with a resident population of Mexican free-tailed bats. The trail opened in 1993 as part of the National Rails-to-Trails program. It's the perfect addition to your stay.

RECOMMENDED READING

"Red River War in the Texas Panhandle" at www.thc.state.tx.us and *The Voice of the Desert: A Naturalist's Interpretation* by Joseph Wood Krutch, 1954.

VOICES FROM THE CAMPFIRE

"When a philosopher's argument becomes tedious, complicated, and opaque, it is usually a sign that he is trying to prove as true to the intellect what is plainly false to common sense. But men of intellect will believe anything—if it appeals to their ego, their vanity, their sense of self-importance" (Edward Abbey, *A Voice Crying in the Wilderness,* 1989).

MAP

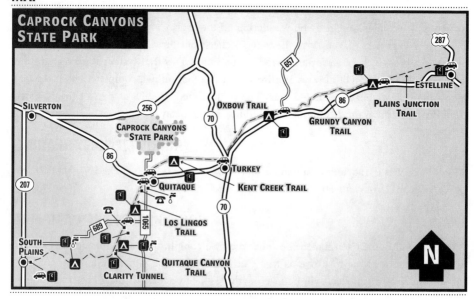

CAPROCK CANYONS STATE PARK

SILVERTON — 256

CAPROCK CANYONS STATE PARK

287

657

ESTELLINE

OXBOW TRAIL

86

PLAINS JUNCTION TRAIL

70

GRUNDY CANYON TRAIL

86

207

QUITAQUE

TURKEY

KENT CREEK TRAIL

70

1065

LOS LINGOS TRAIL

689

SOUTH PLAINS

QUITAQUE CANYON TRAIL

CLARITY TUNNEL

N

GETTING THERE

Off Interstate 27 between
Lubbock and Amarillo,
travel east on TX 86 to the
town of Quitaque. The park
is 3.5 miles north on
FM 1065.

GPS COORDINATES

UTM Zone (WGS84)	14S
Easting	311219
Northing	3809530
Latitude	N 34.4100°
Longitude	W 101.0540°

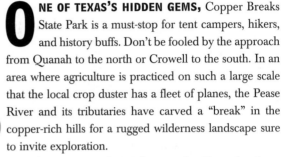

> *On a quiet day, you can easily imagine an early cowboy tending his campfire.*

ONE OF TEXAS'S HIDDEN GEMS, Copper Breaks State Park is a must-stop for tent campers, hikers, and history buffs. Don't be fooled by the approach from Quanah to the north or Crowell to the south. In an area where agriculture is practiced on such a large scale that the local crop duster has a fleet of planes, the Pease River and its tributaries have carved a "break" in the copper-rich hills for a rugged wilderness landscape sure to invite exploration.

As you enter the park, note the Texas longhorn herd on your left and prepare for a real history lesson about the early inhabitants of Texas. At the park's headquarters, there is a small, but exceptional museum telling the story of fierce Comanches who hunted buffalo and protected their land against pioneers for more than 150 years. There is also the story of the legendary Quanah Parker, the last chief of the Staked Plains Comanches, whose Anglo mother was taken as a 9-year-old girl. She eventually married Chief Nocona, and when "found," did not want to leave her Native American family.

As you leave the headquarters and museum, note the warning about being in rattlesnake country and head into the park. As you travel the steep downhill grade of the road, the landscape instantly transforms from a flat prairie to multicolored rock cliffs lining the road; at the bottom, the trees begin to tower overhead. Take an immediate left into Kiowa Camping Area with 11 "civilized" tent sites near the modern restrooms and showers. This well-maintained area is sheltered by the surrounding rocky hillsides and the trees. The center area is more level, but the outer sites, especially site 29, are set back in the brush for more privacy.

Returning to the main road, turn left and follow that road along the cedar-covered cliff with areas where the water could easily pour over the road in a thunderstorm. At the top of the road, go past the RV area and

RATINGS

Beauty: ☆ ☆ ☆ ☆
Privacy: ☆ ☆ ☆
Spaciousness: ☆ ☆ ☆ ☆
Quiet: ☆ ☆ ☆ ☆
Security: ☆ ☆ ☆ ☆
Cleanliness: ☆ ☆ ☆ ☆

scenic overlook on your left. Turn right into the equestrian camp area just off the pavement. These sites 37 through 42 are perched along a canyon with excellent views of the surrounding territory. There are central hitching rails for your horses, but no corrals. On a quiet day, you can easily imagine an early cowboy tending his campfire here while watching the brush for the slightest movement indicating danger. It is also easy to see the Comanche warrior defending this beautiful land where his ancestors had been at home for many years.

Continuing on the paved road, sites 43 through 45 and group site 46 provide some of the premier tent-camping sites in Texas. These breezy wide-open sites sit on a small, elevated peninsula with unrestricted views over the mesas and canyons as far as you can see. They also look down on the Big Pond, where the local birds, deer, coyotes, jackrabbits, and other wildlife meet for life-sustaining water. Be sure to bring binoculars for the best views and a camera for sunsets as spectacular as those enjoyed by the cowboys and Comanches who were here not that long ago.

As you return toward headquarters, turn right into the scenic view area, where the 2-mile Bull Canyon Hiking Trail is located. Be sure to take water anytime of year and watch your step in case any local reptiles are lounging on the pathway. From the scenic viewpoint, you also look down on Lake Copper Breaks where there are two additional trails: 0.5-mile Juniper Ridge Nature Trail and Rocky Ledges Loop. Note that the loop also allows mountain bikes.

Whatever your interest, spend some reflective time at this authentic scene of Texas history.

RECOMMENDED READING

The Man Who Walked Through Time by Colin Fletcher, 1967.

VOICES FROM THE CAMPFIRE

"I wish I knew where I was going. Doomed to be 'carried of the spirit into the wilderness,' I suppose. I wish I could be more moderate in my desires, but I cannot, as so there is no rest" (*The Life and Letters of John Muir,* 1923).

KEY INFORMATION

ADDRESS: Route 2, Box 480 Quanah, TX 79252

OPERATED BY: Texas Parks and Wildlife Dept.

INFORMATION: (817) 839-4331

RESERVATIONS: (512) 389-8900; www.tpwd.state .tx.us

OPEN: All year

SITES: 11 (Kiowa); 10 (Big Pond)

EACH SITE: Picnic table, fire ring, upright grill, lantern hook, water

ASSIGNMENT: Reservations get you in the campground; site choice is first come, first served

REGISTRATION: At headquarters

FACILITIES: Modern restrooms at both areas; showers at Kiowa

PARKING: At each site

FEE: $10; $2 per person entrance fee ages 13 and over; $1 seniors 65 and over

ELEVATION: 1,435 feet

RESTRICTIONS: *Pets:* On leash only *Fires:* In fire rings or grates; check for burn bans *Alcohol:* Prohibited *Vehicles:* 2 per site *Other:* Maximum 8 persons per site; guests must leave by 10 p.m.; quiet time 10 p.m.– 6 a.m.; bring your own firewood or charcoal; limited supplies at headquarters; pick up main supplies in Quanah; gathering firewood prohibited

MAP

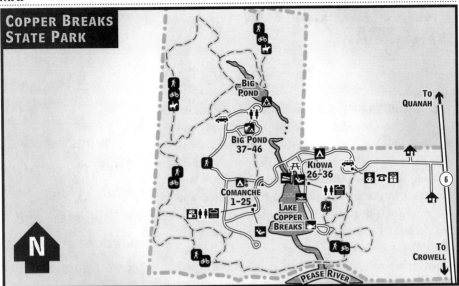

GETTING THERE

From Quanah and US 287, travel 12.7 miles south on TX 6 to PR 62. Turn right. Headquarters is 0.7 miles straight ahead.

GPS COORDINATES

UTM Zone (WGS84)   14S
Easting   431466
Northing   3774813
Latitude   N 34.1119°
Longitude   W 99.7431°

37
PALO DURO CANYON STATE PARK

AS YOU TRAVEL THE PANHANDLE of Texas, the horizons seem limitless and cotton fields surround you in every direction. However, as you approach the entrance of this popular park, the first-time visitor will be pleasantly surprised, if not a little awestruck, by the massive canyon that opens up before you here. Stretching 120 miles and up to 800 feet deep, this geological marvel was formed by the seemingly peaceful Prairie Dog Town fork of the Red River, which crosses the park road at six different places and provides nice wading spots and even a mud bath or two for visitors. At most times of the year, you can cross safely on foot or by car, but a quick look at the flood gauge and the amount of sand piled up by a park bulldozer is a reminder that water is a powerful and dangerous force to be respected.

Leaving the entrance station and descending into the canyon, the scenic overlook and Civilian Conservation Corps (CCC) trailhead is 0.8 miles on your right along with the turnoff to the visitor center and gift shop. Proceeding 2.1 miles down the switchback roadway, you reach the Pioneer Amphitheater, where the outdoor musical extravaganza *Texas* has been playing for more than four decades to packed audiences during cool summer evenings. This classic attraction of the Texas panhandle uses the canyon beauty as a backdrop and is a tradition with many locals and travelers alike. Recently, the production was musically reproduced, and the food served during it was upgraded by the legendary Big Texan Steakhouse for those hungry hikers and campers wishing to complete their Texas experience.

Returning to the main park road, travel 3.2 miles to the Fortress Cliff Camp Area on the right. As you enter the campground, look for secluded site 50 on the far right and then sites 49, 47, 45, 43, and 41 backing up to the heavy canyon vegetation. This tent-site area

> *Surrounding cliffs of bright red claystone, white gypsum, and yellow, gray, and lavender mudstone will keep photographers busy until the last rays of sundown.*

RATINGS

Beauty: ✰ ✰ ✰ ✰
Privacy: ✰ ✰ ✰
Spaciousness: ✰ ✰ ✰
Quiet: ✰ ✰ ✰
Security: ✰ ✰ ✰ ✰
Cleanliness: ✰ ✰ ✰

ADDRESS: Route 2, Box 285
Canyon, TX 79015

OPERATED BY: Texas Parks
and Wildlife Dept.

INFORMATION: (806) 488-2227 or
(806) 488-2506

RESERVATIONS: (512) 389-8900;
www.tpwd.state
.tx.us

OPEN: All year

SITES: 24 tent sites

EACH SITE: Covered picnic
table, fire pit

ASSIGNMENT: Reservations get
you in the camp-
ground; site
choice is first
come, first served

REGISTRATION: At headquarters

FACILITIES: Restrooms and
showers near tent
areas; visitor cen-
ter; park store; sta-
bles; amphitheater

PARKING: At each site

FEE: $12; $4 per person
entrance fee, $2
ages 65 and over,
free ages 12 and
under

ELEVATION: 3,450 feet

RESTRICTIONS: *Pets:* On leash only
Fires: In fire pits
Alcohol: Prohibited
Vehicles: 2 per site
Other: Maximum 8
persons per site;
guests must leave
by 10 p.m.; quiet
time 10 p.m.–
6 a.m.; bring your
own firewood or
charcoal; limited
supplies at park
store located at
The Trading Post;
pick up main sup-
plies in Canyon or
Amarillo; gather-
ing firewood
prohibited

has excellent views of the surrounding cliffs of bright red claystone and white gypsum, along with yellow, gray, and lavender mudstone—all of which will keep the photographers in your group busy until the last rays of a sundown disappear over the canyon rim and the western horizon. With the coming of nighttime, be sure to enjoy the dark skies and the intoxicating smell of a wood fire, which is finally allowed after a summer of burn bans in many Texas parks.

Turning right out of Fortress Cliff, proceed 1.4 miles to the Cactus Camp Area and sites 70 through 76. The park road runs down the middle of these sites and is 0.4 miles before the large Mesquite Camp Area, which has modern restrooms and showers, but is also very popular with RVers and mountain bikers setting up weekend base camp.

While camping at Palo Duro State Park, there are multiple options for outdoor adventure and exercise including hiking, equestrian trails, mountain biking, and even a rugged 11-mile running trail for the more recent athletic pioneer.

From the Mesquite Camp Area, travel the final 0.8 miles to the road's end and the historical marker for the Red River War. This 1874 battle led to the capture of some 1,400 horses that belonged to various Native American tribes who had lived and hunted buffalo on the high plains for multiple generations. The loss of the horses forced the tribes back to the reservations in Oklahoma and allowed Charles Goodnight to eventually run 100,000 head of cattle in the Palo Duro Canyon area. When a large group of Comanches and Kiowas returned in 1878, they found no buffalo remaining and settled for a treaty that allowed for two beef cattle a day until they returned to their reservations, thus ending the era of traditional hunting by the tribes and beginning the legend of the trail drive and the Texas Cowboy.

RECOMMENDED READING

Desert Solitaire by Edward Abbey, 1968.

VOICES FROM THE CAMPFIRE

"No more cars in national parks. Let the people walk. . . . We have agreed not to drive our automobiles into cathedrals, concert halls, art museums, legislative assemblies, private bedrooms and the other sanctums of our culture; we should treat our national parks with the same deference, for they, too, are holy places" (Edward Abbey, *Desert Solitaire,* 1968).

MAP

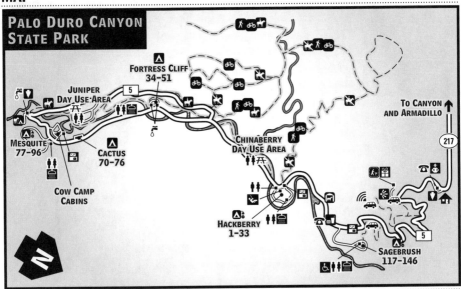

GETTING THERE

From I-25 in Canyon, 12 miles south of Amarillo, proceed 14 miles east on TX 217 to the entrance station and PR 5.

GPS COORDINATES

UTM Zone (WGS84)   14S
Easting   253359
Northing   3874627
Latitude   N 34.9842°
Longitude   W 101.7020°

DEEP EAST TEXAS
AND THE BIG THICKET

38 FAIRFIELD STATE PARK

IF YOU ARE LOOKING FOR A HIDDEN PIECE of Texas wilderness that offers great fishing, hiking, horseback riding, and tent camping without an RV in sight, Fairfield Lake State Park is your destination. Only 8 miles off Interstate 45, the terrain here is a mix of hill country and deep east Texas where sleek vultures are often flying high overhead looking for lunch.

As you approach the entrance station, the Dockery Trail is on the right and parking for the Big Brown Creek Primitive Camping Area is on the left. This 6-mile trail allows hiking, mountain bikes, and horses and ends at primitive tent sites near the lake.

Returning to the main road, enter the park and travel straight ahead on PW 5078 for 1.4 miles past the Fairfield Lake Bird-watching Trail on the left. Continue another 1.6 miles to the Springfield Camping Area on your left, where you will find 36 tent sites shaded by huge oak trees. These well-spaced sites line both sides of the road with sites 14, 16, 18, and 20 backing up to deep forest and offering a feeling of remoteness. Sites 22, 23, 26, 28, and 29 have water views and even prime frontage, depending on the water level. Combined with centrally located restrooms and showers for this tent-only campground, you have a relaxed base for the weekend.

Be sure to note that this popular tent campground is closed from the first part of December until mid-March, so call ahead for reservations and exact opening dates.

Returning to the main road, a left turn takes you to two large camping areas that have not only electricity, but also level tent pads perfect for the local boy scout troop. Look for sites 91 and 93 for some privacy and easy access to a short trail connecting it to Springfield.

Once settled at your site, grab the fishing gear for a wide range of catches, including red drum, crappie, blue tilapia, largemouth bass, and that Texas favorite,

> *Once settled in your site, grab the fishing gear for a wide range of catches.*

RATINGS

Beauty: ✿ ✿ ✿
Privacy: ✿ ✿ ✿
Spaciousness: ✿ ✿ ✿ ✿
Quiet: ✿ ✿ ✿ ✿
Security: ✿ ✿ ✿
Cleanliness: ✿ ✿ ✿

ADDRESS:	123 State Park Road 64 Fairfield, TX 75840
OPERATED BY:	Texas Parks and Wildlife Dept.
INFORMATION:	(903) 389-4514
RESERVATIONS:	(512) 389-8900; www.tpwd.state .tx.us
OPEN:	All year
SITES:	36
EACH SITE:	Picnic table, fire ring, lantern hook
ASSIGNMENT:	Reservations get you in the campground; site choice is first come, first served
REGISTRATION:	At headquarters
FACILITIES:	Modern restrooms and showers
PARKING:	At each site
FEE:	$12 water-only sites; $9 primitive camping; $4 per person entrance fee; $2 ages 65 and older; free for those under age 13 and over age 79
ELEVATION:	362 feet
RESTRICTIONS:	*Pets:* On leash only *Fires:* In fire rings only; check for burn bans *Alcohol:* Prohibited *Vehicles:* 2 per site *Other:* Maximum 8 persons per site; guests must leave by 10 p.m.; quiet time 10 p.m.– 6 a.m.; bring your own firewood or charcoal; limited supplies at park store; main supplies in Fairfield; gathering firewood prohibited

channel catfish (limit 25 per day . . . please). If not fishing, grab a good book, sit back, relax, and enjoy this peaceful park where the main sounds you hear are the birds and the wind.

When you are ready for some exercise, try Big Brown Creek Trail, which starts in the upland region of the post oak savannah region of Texas and ends 2.5 miles later in the flood plain of Big Brown Creek. You'll pass under towering post oaks, blackjack oaks, water oaks, and black hickory and alongside eastern red cedars, yaupons, holly, and American beautyberry as you descend to the creek. As you near the trail's end, look for the primitive camping area if you wish to leave the comforts of the car-camping area behind. A chemical toilet accommodates those who choose to visit this wilder portion of the park.

The other trail is Dockery Trail, which follows the perimeter of the park and is also open to hikers, bikers, and equestrians. It also leaves from the parking lot just outside the park entrance and eventually leads to the lake some 6 miles later. If you have any energy left, the 2-mile nature walk and 1-mile bird-watching trail will finish your day and send you back to your campsite ready for a cold drink and that good book you left unfinished.

Although not well known outside the region, this park is very popular, so make your reservations early.

RECOMMENDED READING

Hiking and Backpacking Trails of Texas by Mickey Little, 1990.

VOICES FROM THE CAMPFIRE

"To live healthily and successfully on the land we must also live with it. We must be part not only of the human community, but of the whole community; we must acknowledge some sort of oneness not only with our neighbors, our countryman but also some respect for the natural as well as for the man-made community" (Joseph Wood Krutch, *The Voice of the Desert,* 1954).

MAP

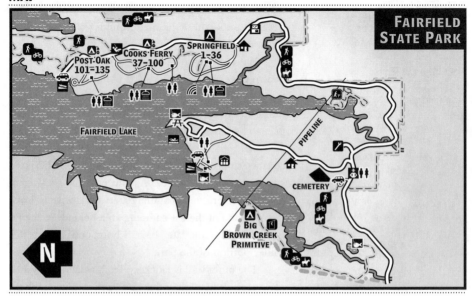

POST OAK
101–135

COOKS FERRY
37–100

SPRINGFIELD
1–36

FAIRFIELD LAKE

PIPELINE

CEMETERY

BIG
BROWN CREEK
PRIMITIVE

N

GETTING THERE

Traveling east of Fairfield on
US 84, turn left on FM 488.
Veer right on FM 2570. Take
a right turn on FM 3285. PR
64 is 3.3 miles straight ahead.

GPS COORDINATES

UTM Zone (WGS84)	14R
Easting	777247
Northing	3518119
Latitude	N 31.7650°
Longitude	W 96.0728°

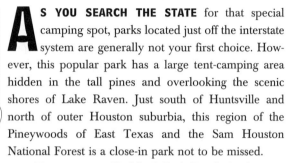

> *Huntsville State Park is a piece of wilderness hidden from the big city.*

AS YOU SEARCH THE STATE for that special camping spot, parks located just off the interstate system are generally not your first choice. However, this popular park has a large tent-camping area hidden in the tall pines and overlooking the scenic shores of Lake Raven. Just south of Huntsville and north of outer Houston suburbia, this region of the Pineywoods of East Texas and the Sam Houston National Forest is a close-in park not to be missed.

Turning west off of I-45, Park Road 40 takes you 1.3 miles into heavy tree cover and quickly leaves the speeding traffic world behind. Signs for "Deer Crossing" and "Alligators exist in the Park" confirm you have left the human habitat and entered an island of wilderness.

As you leave the entrance station, turn left on Park Road 40A toward Coloneh/Raven Hill Camping Areas. With towering pine trees shading the way, go past the Raven Hill RV area and turn right into sites 47 through 58. The lake quickly appears on your right, and premium waterfront sites 57 through 60 have not only clear views of the water but also reflections of spectacular sunset colors behind the distant tree-lined shore.

Continue on to the right for more premium waterfront sites 62 through 64 and 67 through 72, which will fill up quickly. However, even if full, the interior sites are sufficiently elevated to still enjoy the lake.

Travel farther into the Coloneh Camping Area past the fishing pier on your right for another 14 waterfront tent sites with modern restrooms and showers in the circle area. There is also trailhead parking for 13 miles of hiking and biking trails.

Returning to the main road, turn left toward the bathhouse buildings built by one of the few African-American companies of the Civilian Conservation Corps. At this popular day-use spot, you can rent

RATINGS

Beauty: ✿ ✿ ✿ ✿
Privacy: ✿ ✿ ✿
Spaciousness: ✿ ✿ ✿
Quiet: ✿ ✿ ✿
Security: ✿ ✿ ✿
Cleanliness: ✿ ✿ ✿

canoes, kayaks, and flat-bottom boats. Horseback riding is also available, along with a nature center.

After setting up your tent, begin your exploration at the nature center immediately next to the entrance station. This small but functional interpretive center has exhibits about the varied plant life you will encounter on the trail system, including loblolly and shortleaf pines towering over dogwoods flowering in the spring. The park has also allowed most of the understory to remain quite thick and wild enough to hide fox, opossums, white-tailed deer, and wet enough for an occasional alligator.

Trailhead parking is across the street from the nature center and makes an excellent place to begin your hike or even a guided horseback ride. The trail is only moderately difficult but does require sufficient water and snacks if you plan on heading deep into the red maples, dogwoods, and sassafras listening for pileated woodpeckers looking for insects hiding in the tall pine trees overhead. As always, stay on the marked trail to avoid damaging the ecosystem or encountering a healthy patch of poison ivy.

Returning to the main road, continue approximately 1 mile to the park's day-use area for a protected swimming area with a bathhouse on your left. This area is very popular in warm weather and also offers canoe, kayak, and flat-bottom boat rentals in case you want a closer look at the alligators floating motionless in the lake's quiet coves or the great blue herons searching for a snack.

Back at the tent area, build a fire to ward off any chill in the night and watch the sunset reflection in the lake. Just the smell of a fire will push away those big-city thoughts and give you a good night's sleep under the piney woods of Texas.

RECOMMENDED **READING**

Falling from Grace in Texas: A Literary Response to the Demise of Paradise edited by Rick Bass and Paul Christensen, 2004.

KEY INFORMATION

ADDRESS:	P.O. Box 508 Huntsville, TX 77342
OPERATED BY:	Texas Parks and Wildlife Dept.
INFORMATION:	(936) 295-5644
RESERVATIONS:	(512) 389-8900; www.tpwd.state.tx.us
OPEN:	All year
SITES:	87
EACH SITE:	Picnic table, fire ring, lantern hook, central water
ASSIGNMENT:	Reservations get you in the campground; site choice is first come, first served
REGISTRATION:	At headquarters
FACILITIES:	Modern restrooms and showers, boat rentals, nature center, horseback riding
PARKING:	At each site
FEE:	$12; $4 per person entrance fee ages 13 and older; ages 12 and under free
ELEVATION:	432 feet
RESTRICTIONS:	*Pets:* On leash only *Fires:* In fire rings *Alcohol:* Prohibited *Vehicles:* 2 per site *Other:* Maximum 8 persons per site; guests must leave by 10 p.m.; quiet time 10p.m.– 6 a.m.; bring your own firewood or charcoal; limited supplies at park store; pick up main supplies in Huntsville; gathering firewood prohibited.

MAP

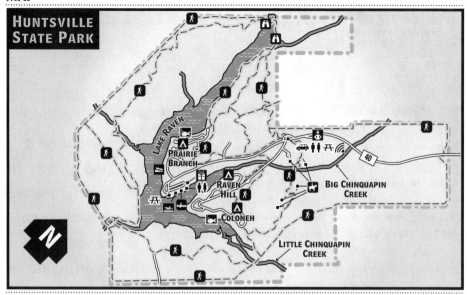

Huntsville State Park

Lake Raven

Prairie Branch

Raven Hill

Coloneh

Big Chinquapin Creek

Little Chinquapin Creek

40

GETTING THERE

Drive 8 miles south of Huntsville on I-45, then 1.3 miles west on Park Road 40.

GPS COORDINATES

UTM Zone (WGS84) 15R
Easting 257875
Northing 3391130
Latitude N 30.6283°
Longitude W 95.5261°

VOICES FROM THE CAMPFIRE

"To waste, to destroy, our natural resources, to skin and exhaust the land instead of using it so as to increase its usefulness, will result in undermining in the days of our children the very prosperity which we ought by right to hand down to them amplified and developed" (President Theodore Roosevelt in a message to Congress in 1907, as quoted by Paul Boller Jr., *Falling from Grace in Texas,* 2004).

40
MARTIN DIES JR. STATE PARK

LOCATED ON THE NORTHERN EDGE of the Big Thicket, this deep east Texas park combines the best of open waters on B. A. Steinhagen Reservoir and extensive wilderness swamp areas. You can rent canoes or bring your own boat for a close-up view of one of the premier natural areas in the country, where you might see alligators, roadrunners, and numerous deer appearing like ghosts out of the dense underbrush at dusk.

As you approach on US 190, the park is split into the Hen House Ridge Unit to the south and the Walnut Ridge Unit to the north. The main headquarters is to the south on PR 48. Continue straight over the bridge, where you get your first good look at the rugged backwater of the Gum Slough, until you reach premier waterfront tent-camping sites 36 through 38 and 39 through 45. The views here are great and have a protected swimming area nearby in the day-use area. The interior sites are a little larger and still have a lake view with room to spread out in the grassy meadow. Turning the corner away from the lake leads to the interior sites 67 through 79, in case the other sites are not available.

Returning toward headquarters, don't miss the 2.2-mile slough trail on your right for great photography spots and solitude. Note that this trail returns to PR 48 just a short distance from the 1.1-mile Forest Trail, so take along water and keep a sharp lookout for any resident reptiles that might be using the trail at the same time as you. If you don't want to go alone, there are guided interpretive walks from the headquarters.

Back in your auto, return to US 190, turn left, and then make an immediate right turn on North PR 48 toward the Walnut Ridge Unit. While you will want to visit the Nature Center, the Wildscape Herb Garden, and the 1.5-mile Wildlife Trail, the real attraction is the wilderness feel of hanging moss and the low-water

> *Here you'll get a close-up view of one of the premier natural areas in the country, where you might see alligators, roadrunners and numerous deer appearing like ghosts out of the dense under-brush at dusk.*

RATINGS

Beauty: ✩ ✩ ✩ ✩
Privacy: ✩ ✩ ✩
Spaciousness: ✩ ✩ ✩
Quiet: ✩ ✩ ✩
Security: ✩ ✩ ✩ ✩
Cleanliness: ✩ ✩ ✩ ✩

sloughs near the roadway. At 0.7 miles past the entrance station, make a right turn for premier tent-camping sites 102 through 104. While these large sites do not have water, their remote location and immediate access to the 0.8-mile Island Trail and a long boardwalk connecting to the 0.4-mile Loop Trail provide excellent sunrise and sunset photography or bird-watching opportunities.

Returning to the main road, go past the shelter area and turn right on the one-way road toward sites 105 through 182. Site 107 on your far right is in the RV area but provides a perfect sunset view over the water. Continue through the RV area to tent sites 125 through 131. Huge trees shade this area, and site 125 has the lake on one side and the slough on the other. Sites 126 through 132 back up to the slough for that up-close experience of the Big Thicket.

Leaving the park, head south to the patchwork of wilderness areas that make up the 100,000-acre Big Thicket National Preserve. Start at the visitor center on US 69 south of Woodville and bring your hiking boots, cameras, and day packs to enjoy more than 45 miles of hiking trails and a unique mix of plants—such as cacti and yucca plants—that coexist with the swamps and cypress trees.

While in the area, check out Village Creek State Park for tent-camping opportunities, but be sure to call ahead, (512) 389-8900, to determine availability after hurricanes recently decided to hammer this already wild and untamed portion of deep east Texas. Even if you can't tent camp, there is still canoeing on this free-flowing tributary of the Neches River, whose very existence is threatened by the large urban area's thirst for another reservoir site.

RECOMMENDED READING

The Big Thicket: An Ecological Reevaluation by Pete A.Y. Gunter, 1993.

MAP

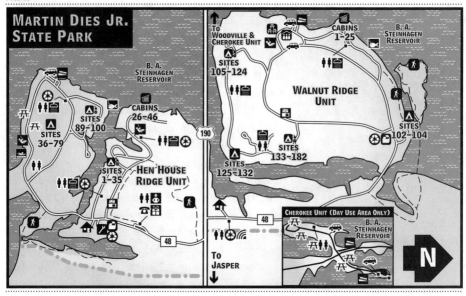

VOICES FROM THE CAMPFIRE

"It is really no exaggeration to say that the Big Thicket is the Biological Crossroads of North America. It contains both temperate and subtropical plants and animals, along with many from the dry, treeless west. In the Thicket there are many varieties of orchids; but there are also species of sage-brush and cacti. In few other places will one find roadrunners alongside alligators, mesquite alongside cypress and water tupelo" (Pete A.Y. Gunter, *The Big Thicket: An Ecological Reevaluation*, 1993).

GETTING THERE

From Jasper, travel 10 miles west on US 190. From Woodville, travel 15 miles east on US 190. PR 48 is on both sides of the road.

GPS COORDINATES

UTM Zone (WGS84)	15R
Easting	388524
Northing	3413161
Latitude	N 30.8464°
Longitude	W 94.1658°

> *These spacious sites follow the shoreline for premium waterfront camping and 180-degree views.*

FOR ALL THOSE TENT CAMPERS who pour over their maps and search out little-known roads leading to the most remote locations, Rayburn Park is a must-stop. Leaving Pineland on FR 83 West, cross the Ayish Bayou and enter the Angelina National Forest. Take FR 705 South into the towering pines and notice the various hunting clubs on your left hanging onto the remaining wildlands threatened by the clear-cutters.

A right turn on South Spur 3127 and then a left on South Spur 3127 qualifies as being officially off-the-tourist route, but the location is a great tent campground. After passing the gatehouse and visiting the friendly staff, the first right leads to tent sites 1 through 10 in the shelter of huge pine trees and lake views on both sides of the road. Check out sites 2, 3, and 4 if you want a personal boat ramp. The other sites are quieter in summer season.

Returning to the main road, continue to the end veering right for the RV area with new modern restrooms, showers, and awe-inspiring sunset views over the 114,000-acre lake. Veer to the left for tent-camping sites 55 through 65. These spacious sites follow the shoreline for premium waterfront camping and 180-degree views. Continue around the corner, and site 65 on the end has maximum privacy and tree cover plus a little shelter on windy days.

After leaving this park, don't forget to visit the other Corps of Engineer parks located around the 750 miles of shoreline. Tent campers will find two excellent choices: Twin Dikes and Ebenezer. Both of these parks are located off FM 255 on the south side of the reservoir. Whichever park you choose, enjoy yourself in the towering east Texas pines and on the water.

As you travel around this massive reservoir, you soon learn that timber is a crop to the local timber companies, and conflicts with conservationists are not

RATINGS

Beauty: ✿ ✿ ✿ ✿
Privacy: ✿ ✿ ✿
Spaciousness: ✿ ✿ ✿
Quiet: ✿ ✿ ✿
Security: ✿ ✿ ✿
Cleanliness: ✿ ✿ ✿ ✿

easily resolved. The good news is that sport hunters and fishermen have now realized that the harvesting of trees and the bulldozers that follow are destroying the wildlife they depend on. Without habitat protection, the fish, deer, and game birds will eventually disappear. Tent campers have long known that clear-cutting is a threat to not only wildlife but also the very wilderness they search for as a place of solitude. With the new alliances between the traditional hunting, fishing, and conservation groups, there is some hope that major wilderness areas will be saved.

Returning to your campsite, pull up a chair and read a good book or simply gaze on the seemingly endless miles of waterway. You can also launch your canoe or kayak for a closer inspection of the shoreline, but beware of high winds if you venture out too far. Of course, if you brought your sailboat, Sam Rayburn Reservoir will reward you with many hours of wide-open cruising, powered by nature, and leaving no footprints

RECOMMENDED READING

Clearcutting: A Crime Against Nature by Edward C. Fritz, 1989.

VOICES FROM THE CAMPFIRE

"A clearcut looks like a war zone. It is the radical surgery of the timber business. The soil washes off like blood" (Edward C. Fritz, *Clearcutting: A Crime Against Nature,* 1989).

KEY INFORMATION

ADDRESS:	Route 3, Box 486 Jasper, TX 75951
OPERATED BY:	U.S. Army Corps of Engineers
INFORMATION:	(409) 384-5716
RESERVATIONS:	(877) 444-6777
OPEN:	All year
SITES:	24
EACH SITE:	Picnic table, fire ring, central water
ASSIGNMENT:	Reservations get you in the campground; site choice is first come, first served
REGISTRATION:	At the gatehouse
FACILITIES:	Modern restrooms and showers in RV area; vault restrooms in tent-camping areas; boat ramp
PARKING:	At each site
FEE:	$11
ELEVATION:	301 feet
RESTRICTIONS:	*Pets:* On leash only *Fires:* In fire rings only; check on burn bans *Alcohol:* Prohibited *Vehicles:* 2 per site *Other:* Maximum 8 persons per site; guests must leave by 10 p.m.; quiet time 10 p.m.– 6 a.m.; bring your own firewood or charcoal; pick up main supplies in Pineland; gathering firewood prohibited

MAP

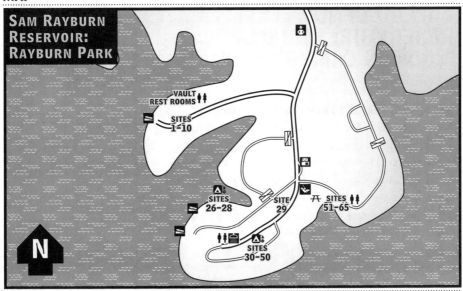

SAM RAYBURN
RESERVOIR:
RAYBURN PARK

VAULT
REST ROOMS

SITES
1-10

SITES
26-28

SITE
29

SITES
51-65

SITES
30-50

N

GETTING THERE

From Pineland, travel 22
miles west on FR 83. Then
travel 11 miles south on
FR 705 to South Spur 3127.
Take a right turn on South
Spur 3127 to find the
park entrance.

GPS COORDINATES

UTM Zone (WGS84)   15R
Easting   394447
Northing   3442353
Latitude   N 31.1103°
Longitude   W 94.1069°

42
TOLEDO BEND RESERVOIR: INDIAN MOUNDS CAMPGROUND

AS YOU TRAVEL 7 MILES EAST from Hemphill on Farm Road 83, a right turn on Farm Road 3382 leads to a dense forest drive running along the border of the 11,037-acre Indian Mounds Wilderness Area. This rugged part of the Sabine National Forest prohibits any motorized access, and only hikers or equestrian riders may enter the area. Backpacking and primitive camping are also allowed, but do be careful in hunting season.

After the pay station, the road narrows and the trees form a canopy down the long hill toward the water. Deep ravines on both sides are filled with flowering redbuds and dogwoods. A right turn on the Crazy Horse Camping Loop begins with site 25 on the right and continues with spacious sites and large, level tent pads. Site 31 has a great view of the inlet area where fishing boats drift with the winds searching for that perfect spot. The entire campground is shaded by huge pines, including site 36, which is a great tent site down a small hill next to a dry creek. Even if you have to drive for a shower, this is rustic tent camping at its best.

Returning to the park road, make a right turn and then an immediate left into Buffalo Hide Campground. This loop road has 24 sites, all with a lake view. Proceed to sites 9, 10, 12, 14, and 16 for premier waterfront properties sheltered by huge pine trees. They offer excellent vantage points for observing the local wildlife, including, perhaps, a brief glimpse of the exotic red-plumed male pileated woodpecker.

As a final stop on the main road, a left turn takes you to the boat ramp for unlimited fishing opportunities along 1,200 miles of shoreline. Continue straight ahead to the Arrowhead Camping Loop, where there are no tables, no water, and no restrooms. However, it doesn't matter, because these primitive campsites are located on an elevated peninsula providing spectacular

> *This is rustic tent camping at its best.*

RATINGS

Beauty: ✿ ✿ ✿ ✿
Privacy: ✿ ✿ ✿
Spaciousness: ✿ ✿ ✿
Quiet: ✿ ✿ ✿
Security: ✿ ✿ ✿
Cleanliness: ✿ ✿ ✿

ADDRESS: Route 1 Box 270 Burkeville, TX 75932

OPERATED BY: Sabine River Authority of Texas

INFORMATION: (409) 565-2273; www.sra.dst.tx.us

RESERVATIONS: None

OPEN: All year

SITES: 35

EACH SITE: Picnic table, lantern hook, fire ring, central water

ASSIGNMENT: First come, first served

REGISTRATION: At self-pay station

FACILITIES: Boat ramp, portable toilets

PARKING: At each site

FEE: $4

ELEVATION: 232 feet

RESTRICTIONS: *Pets:* On leash only *Fires:* In fire rings only *Alcohol:* Prohibited *Vehicles:* 2 per site *Other:* Maximum 8 persons per site; guests must leave by 10 p.m.; quiet time 10 p.m.–7 a.m.; bring your own firewood or charcoal; pick up main supplies in Hemphill; gathering firewood prohibited

180-degree views of the massive reservoir and the state of Louisiana on the far shore.

After choosing your site, head to the 185,000-acre reservoir for one of Texas's premier fishing locations. A boat will allow access to countless coves and inlets where you can fish, bird-watch, or just float with the breeze. If you want a little exercise with your boating, take your canoe or kayak below Toledo Bend Dam for a 54-mile section that runs from the dam to US 190. This section of the Sabine River is very scenic and is only crossed by one road. Numerous white sand bars provide primitive campsites and day-use areas. Look for numerous birds, such as the endangered red-cockaded woodpecker, quail, and eastern wild turkey.

If hiking is your main interest, return to Indian Mounds Wilderness Area on FM 3382 or to Lake View Campground 16 miles southeast of Hemphill via TX 87 and FSR 105. This small campground has ten tent sites and is at the trailhead for the Trail Between the Lakes. This 28-mile hiking trail extends from Lakeview Campground to US 96 within sight of the easternmost point of Sam Rayburn Reservoir. The trail is the result of cooperation between The Sierra Club and the U.S. Forest Service and passes through Moore Plantation Wildlife Management Area and several colonies of red-cockaded woodpeckers. Be sure to check with the local forest-service office as to camping restrictions in these areas, especially during hunting season. The trail is open to hikers only, so your wilderness experience should be excellent. Bring your binoculars and fishing gear to this easternmost park for a great tent camping experience.

RECOMMENDED READING

Adventures with a Texas Naturalist by Roy Bedichek, 1947.

MAP

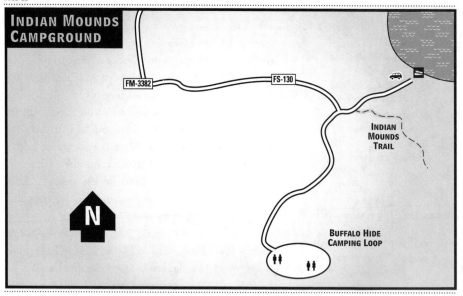

INDIAN MOUNDS CAMPGROUND

FM-3382   FS-130

INDIAN MOUNDS TRAIL

N

BUFFALO HIDE CAMPING LOOP

VOICES **FROM THE CAMPFIRE**

"A stationary camp is quickly cluttered up. Stay too long or return to the same camping place too often, and the inevitable encrustation appears. You fix up a cupboard, install a bench between two trees, improvise a table. These and other little conveniences may be nothing more than a few pimples, but they indicate that the disease of civilization is setting in" (Roy Bedichek, *Adventures with a Texas Naturalist,* 1947).

GETTING **THERE**

From Hemphill, take FR 83 for 7 miles east. Turn right on FR 3382 and drive for 3.9 miles. Turn left into Indian Mounds Recreation Area.

GPS **COORDINATES**

UTM Zone (WGS84)   15R
Easting   433631
Northing   3464656
Latitude   N 31.3144°
Longitude   W 93.6975°

43
TOLEDO BEND RESERVOIR: RAGTOWN RECREATION AREA

Ragtown is not your typical lake campground.

LEAVING THE FAST-GROWING CITY of Lufkin, the creature comforts of fast food and modern mall life disappear in a hurry. They are replaced by the tall pines, flowering redbuds, and dogwoods as you move into a part of Deep East Texas visited only by locals and the lucky tent camper searching for that perfect outdoor experience. Your quest takes you across the Angelina River, through the Angelina National Forest, and into the Sabine River Basin.

At the town of Milam, a left turn on TX 87 takes you toward Ragtown Recreation Area. Heading north on 87, this scenic road roughly parallels the massive reservoir hidden to the east. As you approach Ragtown Recreation Area, you find very quickly this is not the typical lake campground, but a rugged piece of territory marked by massive pine trees and steep ravines. It is a reminder of the difference between a tree farm and a forest with a mix of pines, hardwoods, and understory plants. There is even an area for the critically endangered red-cockaded woodpecker. The 20-year legal fight over this bird helped save much of the national forest from clear-cutting.

After paying at the self-registration station, you enter Ragtown on the narrow road that leads down the hill to the water's edge and boat ramp to the right. Stay straight for the camping area and the camp-host site on your right, along with site 1, which backs up to a heavily wooded ravine, has a nice view of the water, and is across the street from one of the only water sources. Just up the hill are the modern restrooms and showers on the left.

Continue up the hill for more heavily treed sites, including a number of double sites. At the top of the hill are some of the premier tent sites in Texas. On the left side, just after more modern restrooms, look for sites 11 through 14, 16, 19, 21, and 22 for spectacular

RATINGS

Beauty: ☆ ☆ ☆ ☆
Privacy: ☆ ☆ ☆
Spaciousness: ☆ ☆ ☆
Quiet: ☆ ☆ ☆
Security: ☆ ☆ ☆
Cleanliness: ☆ ☆ ☆

views out over the Toledo Bend Reservoir. These elevated sites also allow for some breeze and a little relief from the hot weather of summer. At road's end, there is a small circle drive and an unnumbered spot (probably 25), which puts your tent out on a small peninsula for 180-degree views. The site is level with the water's edge, which is only a short walk down the hill.

When you add easy access to Mother Nature's Trail, the lack of electricity or water at every site is really no problem to the tent camper looking for a perfect Deep East Texas destination. One-mile Mother Nature's Trail loops around the campground and provides great views of the north end of Toledo Bend Reservoir's 185,000 surface acres and its 65 miles of open water. After you pick your tent site, return to the bottom of the hill and head to the water. The world-class fishing includes black bass and crappie. There are also numerous photography options, including sunrise shots over the lake, and bird-watching of all types. In addition to the endangered red-cockaded woodpecker, the area includes bald eagles, ospreys, cranes, herons, hawks, owls, and even a few loons and pelicans on the southern end of the reservoir. Fall is especially beautiful, as the mix of oak, maple, sycamore, cypress, and hickory trees provide bright yellows and deep reds in contrast with the towering pines.

As you leave the campground, take time to visit the small communities of Milam and Geneva, which were stops on the El Camino Real, Texas's oldest trail and highway. The El Camino Real was first used by the Caddo Indians, then by French and Spanish explorers, and finally by a flood of new Texans, including Stephen F. Austin.

RECOMMENDED READING

Texas Land Ethics by Pete A.Y. Gunter and Max Oelschlaeger, 1997.

KEY INFORMATION

ADDRESS:	Route 1, Box 270 Burkeville, TX 75932
OPERATED BY:	Sabine River Authority of Texas
INFORMATION:	(409) 565-2273; www.sra.dst.tx.us
RESERVATIONS:	None
OPEN:	All year
SITES:	25
EACH SITE:	Picnic table, upright fire grate or ring, lantern hook
ASSIGNMENT:	First come, first served
REGISTRATION:	At self-pay station
FACILITIES:	Modern restrooms and showers; boat ramp
PARKING:	At each site
FEE:	Single site, $5; double site, $8
ELEVATION:	305 feet
RESTRICTIONS:	*Pets:* On leash only *Fires:* In fire grates or rings only *Alcohol:* Prohibited *Vehicles:* 2 per site *Other:* Maximum 8 persons per site; guests must leave by 10 p.m.; quiet time 10 p.m.– 6 a.m.; bring firewood or charcoal; pick up main supplies in Center, Logansport, or Hemphill; gathering firewood prohibited

MAP

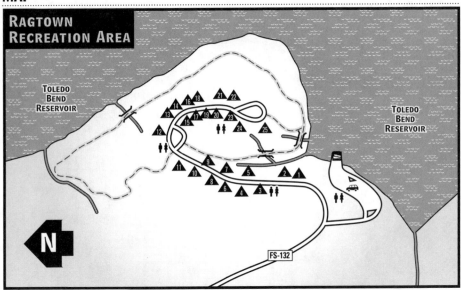

GETTING THERE

Drive 56 miles east of Lufkin on TX 103 to Milam. Drive north 23 miles on TX 87. Take a right turn on FM 139 to FM 3184. Ragtown is 4 miles ahead.

GPS COORDINATES

UTM Zone (WGS84)   15R
Easting   421569
Northing   3505575
Latitude   N 31.6828°
Longitude   W 93.8275°

VOICES FROM THE CAMPFIRE

"Any fool can destroy trees. They cannot run away; and if they could, they would still be destroyed—chased and hunted down as long as fun or a dollar could be got out of their bark hides, branching horns, or magnificent bole backbones. . . . God has cared for these trees, saved them from drought, disease, avalanches, and a thousand straining, leveling tempests and floods; but He cannot save them from fools—only Uncle Sam can do that" (John Muir, 1897).

NORTHEAST TEXAS
AND CADDO LAKE AREA

AS YOU TRAVEL NORTHEAST from the traffic jams of Dallas and its booming suburbs, the rolling countryside of TX 121 is a welcome relief. The trees begin to outnumber the cars and the spaciousness of rural Texas allows you to relax your grip on the steering wheel. Before you reach Bonham, turn right on FM 1629 for 2.9 miles, then left on Texas 78 for 0.9 miles, then left on FM 271. The roadside gets wilder for 3 miles until you reach Park Road 24 and the entrance on your left. The small entrance station is straight ahead and you begin to proceed into a canopy of huge trees shading the road. At 0.4 miles, you cross the Lake Loop bike trail, so be sure to watch for mountain bikers. At 0.7 miles, you'll spot a large, group tent-camping area on the right with multiple picnic tables, upright grills, and central water.

At the intersection, turn left and the tent-only sites are on your immediate left. Starting with site 21, this small campground has a nice view of the lake. Site 20 is set back into the trees for extra privacy. Sites 15 through 19 are also in the trees but are located a little closer to RV sites 1 through 14. These RV sites have electricity hookups if your tent-camping group needs a little modern comfort. The relatively new restrooms and showers (even heated) are a short walk up the road on the right, and park headquarters is on the left in a stone building built by the Civilian Conservation Corps in the 1930s. It has not only a commanding view of the lake but also a large covered pavilion perfect for family reunions or other large groups. This pavilion also sits lakeside with easy access to the fishing pier and provides an ideal view of the resident Canadian snow geese enjoying the breeze and open water.

After setting up your tent, get your hiking boots on or tune up the mountain bike for 11 miles of trails which disappear into the heavy woods. These bike trails offer moderate difficulty and require helmets for safety. You

> *Visit the lakeside pavilion here for a possible glimpse of resident Canadian snow geese enjoying the breeze and open water.*

RATINGS

Beauty: ✰ ✰ ✰
Privacy: ✰ ✰
Spaciousness: ✰ ✰
Quiet: ✰ ✰
Security: ✰ ✰ ✰
Cleanliness: ✰ ✰ ✰ ✰

should also carry plenty of water for proper hydration in the Texas heat. Luckily, the park contains mature stands of Shumard oaks, green ashes, cottonwoods, and mighty oaks to provide shade for hikers and bikers.

After working hard on the trails, head for the small but scenic 65-acre lake, which has a swimming area and canoe and paddleboat rentals. The lake provides a tranquil background for a relaxing afternoon with a good book or fishing off the pier.

As you leave this central area, cross the one-lane bridge for a 0.4-mile scenic return drive to the entrance station. Follow signs back to Bonham for a taste of Texas hospitality, and be sure to visit the Sam Rayburn Library. This Texas legend held power in Washington with the likes of LBJ and FDR.

RECOMMENDED READING

Encounters with the Archdruid by John McPhee, 1971. (Narratives about a conservationist and three of his natural enemies.)

VOICES FROM THE CAMPFIRE

"Conservation is an Inseparable Ingredient of lasting peace and security, and of the economics of peaceful stability. There is surely an economically feasible route to a sustainable society, one that does not over-tax the environment and thus drive civilization to the final quarrel over vanishing resources" (David Brower, *The Fate and Hope of the Earth*, 1991).

MAP

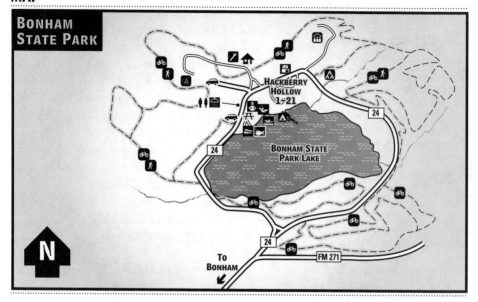

GETTING THERE

From Dallas, travel North on US 75. Take TX 121 toward Bonham and turn right on FM 1629. After 2.9 miles, turn left on TX 78. After 0.9 miles, turn right on FM 271. Park Road 234 is 2 miles on the left.

GPS COORDINATES

UTM Zone (WGS84)   14S
Easting   764607
Northing   3715136
Latitude   N 33.5431°
Longitude   W 96.1503°

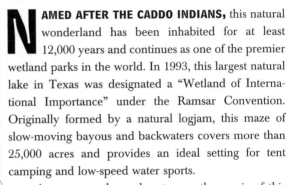

> *Caddo Lake offers large sites with views of the lake that are only enhanced by the hanging moss and huge cypress trees.*

NAMED AFTER THE CADDO INDIANS, this natural wonderland has been inhabited for at least 12,000 years and continues as one of the premier wetland parks in the world. In 1993, this largest natural lake in Texas was designated a "Wetland of International Importance" under the Ramsar Convention. Originally formed by a natural logjam, this maze of slow-moving bayous and backwaters covers more than 25,000 acres and provides an ideal setting for tent camping and low-speed water sports.

As you pass the park entrance, the magic of this place appears almost immediately in the form of thick forests of pine, oak and hickory draped with Spanish moss. Following the main park road for about 1.5 miles, you descend a steep hill and then turn left at the T-intersection toward the camping areas. At the central parking area, stay to your right and cross the wooden bridge into Mill Pond Camping Area for one of Texas's best tent-camping areas. With the lake at your back door, sites 65, 64, and 63 are to your immediate right. These large sites have views of the lake that are only enhanced by the hanging moss and huge cypress trees growing in the shallow water. Proceeding farther, sites 62 through 57 are at the turnaround point and provide the most privacy and solitude. The remaining sites are a little closer together, but the setting has such beauty that even some togetherness is no real distraction, especially on a moonlit walk to the fishing pier just off the central parking area. If the hanging moss and swamp flowers don't give you a feeling of wilderness, then just remember there are alligators in the area, along with 70 species of fish.

Leaving Mill Pond, the concession store is on your left. There you can rent canoes or take a pontoon boat tour. The restrooms and showers are on your right near the entrance to the RV areas and the one-way exit

RATINGS

Beauty: ✿ ✿ ✿ ✿
Privacy: ✿ ✿ ✿
Spaciousness: ✿ ✿ ✿
Quiet: ✿ ✿ ✿
Security: ✿ ✿ ✿
Cleanliness: ✿ ✿ ✿

road. Follow this road 0.2 miles up the hill and make a left toward the boat ramp. Look for the Caddo Forest Trail on your right, which is listed as a 0.75-mile nature walk, but connects to a series of steep hikes and eventually to the old Civilian Conservation Corps Pavilion. The pavilion was built in the 1930s by rugged youths caught in the Great Depression. The trail also ends in a parking and picnic area with great views of the Big Cypress Bayou. Following the one-way road returns you to the central parking area for Mill Pond and the concession store.

Be sure to give yourself a little extra time at Caddo to soak up the natural beauty and rich history. After the Caddo Indians, the area became a sort of hideout for renegades and misfits whose contempt for the law (especially during Prohibition) has become a local tradition. The lake was also a stop on the steamboat route from New Orleans to Jefferson, which explains how this transplanted piece of French architecture landed deep in the Texas piney woods.

So stay awhile and let the tranquil waters soothe those city nerves. You won't regret it.

RECOMMENDED READING

In Wilderness Is the Preservation of the World by Eliot Porter, 1962. (Text from Henry David Thoreau; introduction by David Brower.)

VOICES FROM THE CAMPFIRE

"We can never have enough of nature. We must be refreshed by the sight on inexhaustible vigor, vast and titanic features, the sea-coast with its wrecks, the wilderness with its living and its decaying trees, the thunder cloud, and the rain which lasts three weeks and produces freshets. We need to witness our own limits transgressed, and some life pasturing freely where we never wander" (Henry David Thoreau, *Walden*, 1854).

KEY INFORMATION

ADDRESS:	245 Park Road 2 Karnack, TX 75661
OPERATED BY:	Texas Parks and Wildlife Dept.
INFORMATION:	(903) 679-3351
RESERVATIONS:	(512)389-8900; www.tpwd.state .tx.us
OPEN:	All year
SITES:	20
EACH SITE:	Water, fire ring, picnic table, lantern hook
ASSIGNMENT:	Reservations get you in the campground; site choice is first come, first served
REGISTRATION:	At headquarters
FACILITIES:	Restrooms and showers, canoe rentals and tours, pontoon boat tours, park store, recreation hall
PARKING:	At each site
FEES:	Tent camping $8 per night at Mill Pond; entrance fee $2 per person
ELEVATION:	275 feet
RESTRICTIONS:	*Pets:* On leash only *Fires:* In fire rings *Alcohol:* Prohibited *Vehicles:* 2 per site *Other:* Maximum 8 persons per site; guests must leave by 10 p.m.; quiet time 10 p.m.– 6 a.m.; bring your own firewood or charcoal; limited supplies at concession store at Saw Mill Pond; main supplies in Marshall or Jefferson; gathering firewood prohibited

MAP

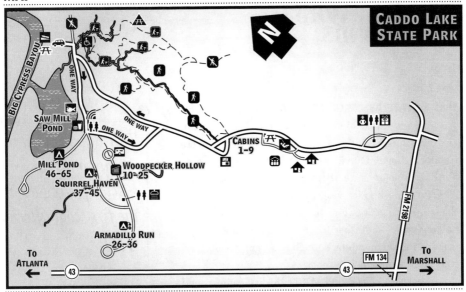

CADDO LAKE STATE PARK

Big Cypress Bayou

Saw Mill Pond

ONE WAY

Mill Pond
46-65

Squirrel Haven
37-45

Woodpecker Hollow
10-25

Armadillo Run
26-36

Cabins
1-9

To
Atlanta

To
Marshall

FM 134

FM 2198

GETTING THERE

In the city of Marshall on
US 59, turn right on TX 43
and drive 14 miles. Turn
right on FM 2198 and go
0.5 miles. Turn left on Park
Road 2; park entrance is
straight ahead.

GPS COORDINATES

UTM Zone (WGS84)   15S
Easting   389679
Northing   3616424
Latitude   N 32.6800°
Longitude   W 94.1767°

46
CADDO NATIONAL GRASSLANDS

IN A STATE AS LARGE AS TEXAS, the hidden gems are exactly that: hidden. This series of three campgrounds is easily overlooked in the 17,873-acre Caddo National Grasslands. While the massive area north of Bonham is clearly marked on state road maps, its very name implies vast, open savannahs with little shade or protection for the tent camper. However, nothing could be further from the truth in this heavily wooded forest containing enough lakes and creeks for a wilderness experience.

After turning east on FM 409, the first campground is Bois D'Arc Trailhead Overnight Area 2.4 miles on the right. The self-pay station and compost toilets are straight ahead, with the campsite loop starting to the right. This heavily treed campground is the prime meeting place for the local equestrian community, whose horse trailers and friendly Texans fill the sites on weekends. This area is the starting point for five different trail loops totaling 28 miles through the rugged Caddo Wildlife Management Area. You might encounter red and gray fox, gulls, quail, white-tailed deer, wild turkey, and two-legged deer hunters in season, so be alert. Site 15 is at the far end of the 0.6-mile loop and offers extra space and privacy but a long walk to the toilet.

Returning to FM 409, turn right for 1.7 miles and then right into Coffeemill Lake Recreation Area. This campground offers lake views from every site, and all sites are nicely spaced. There is a boat ramp, and the large trees give plenty of welcome shade. Sites 12 and 13 are close enough to be called lakefront, but there are no bad places in this small park to put your tent and do a little fishing or just relaxing.

Returning to FM 409, turn right and travel 3 miles to the West Lake Crockett Campground, which is surrounded on three sides by water. This small, ten-site campground is perfectly placed to get the lake breeze

> *Tall pines mixed with mighty oaks take on a special feeling during the first cool afternoons of fall.*

RATINGS

Beauty: ☆ ☆ ☆
Privacy: ☆ ☆ ☆
Spaciousness: ☆ ☆ ☆
Quiet: ☆ ☆ ☆
Security: ☆ ☆
Cleanliness: ☆ ☆ ☆

KEY INFORMATION

and unparalleled views at sunrise or sunset. The tall pines mixed with the mighty oaks take on a special feeling during the first cool afternoons of fall, when the leaves are turning and beginning to cover the ground. The summer crowds have gone home and you are left to enjoy a moment of solitude in this little-known corner of Northeast Texas.

After you select your site, head out on Bois D'Arc Trail for some wilderness hiking or a cross-country equestrian adventure. The topography is moderately strenuous, so bring sufficient food and water to be out all day. You should also check with the local US Forest Service office as to any areas open during hunting season or specific trails that cross some of the remaining patchwork of private property. As you enjoy this great trail system, look for some really nice natural areas near Coffee Mill Creek, which eventually ends in Coffee Mill Lake.

Returning to the Bois D'Arc trailhead, take your fishing gear over to Coffee Mill Lake or West Lake Crockett for some peace and quiet. These small campgrounds are the perfect locations to throw in a line and read a good book. Add in a small fire and you have a great escape from the big city.

RECOMMENDED READING

Of Men and Mountains by William O. Douglas, 1950.

VOICES FROM THE CAMPFIRE

"These fires at night brought cheer and fellowship. We would talk of the happenings of the day and of the plans for tomorrow; of the perplexing problems of school and of home. . . . As the sparks rose to the tops of the trees and disappeared into the firmament, we would dream dreams that only boys can dream" (William O. Douglas, *The Campfire*, 1950).

MAP

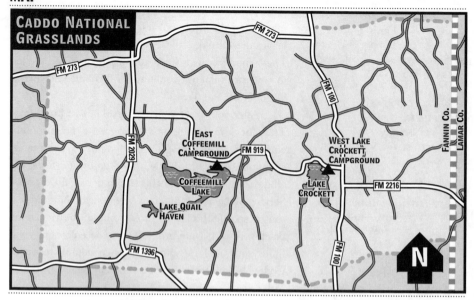

From Telephone, take FM 2029 South 1 mile to FM 409 and turn left. Bois D'Arc is on the right. From Bonham, drive north 6 miles on TX 78 and turn right on FM 1396. Drive 9 miles and turn left on FM 2029. After 3.9 miles, turn right on FM 409. Bois D'Arc is on the right.

GPS COORDINATES

UTM Zone (WGS84)	15S
Easting	224529
Northing	3736901
Latitude	N 33.7364°
Longitude	W 95.9733°

> *Each site has its own private trail and feels more like a backpacking experience.*

ANOTHER **HIDDEN GEM** in the Texas State Park system lies off the beaten tourist path, but should not be missed by avid tent campers. Located on the south shore of Cooper Lake, the South Sulphur Unit offers the usual park activities, but the huge, 19,300-acre lake and more than 25 miles of shoreline give a wilderness feel to all visitors, but especially the tent camper.

After leaving the entrance station, the park road winds through thick stands of oak trees and rolling hills. With each mile, the terrain gets a little wilder until you pass the Buggy Whip Equestrian Camping Area 2.3 miles on your left and enter the Deer Haven RV area. Just as you pass the restrooms and showers on your left, watch for the sign on your right for Oak Grove Camping Area. After parking in the paved central parking area, grab your gear and follow the easy trail to some of the best tent camping around.

Beginning with site number 88 on your far right, each site has its own private trail and feels more like a backpacking experience. Sites 92, 94 through 99, and 101 and 102 are waterfront property where you can hear the waves from your sleeping bag. Most of the sites are divided by heavy brush for extra privacy, but even if you can see a fellow tent camper, you each realize this is a haven of solitude where you can leave your big-city worries behind.

At the end of the trail, sites 99 and 101 even share their own beach. The entire campground is arranged on a peninsula, so you are separate from the RV areas and also have great sunrise or sunset views depending on your final site selection. There are no bathrooms in the Oak Grove campground, but enough nature to wander into as necessary with the restrooms and showers less than 5 minutes away by car.

As you leave the Oak Grove Area, check out the Buggy Whip Equestrian Area and its 11-mile trail.

RATINGS

Beauty: ✫ ✫ ✫ ✫
Privacy: ✫ ✫ ✫ ✫
Spaciousness: ✫ ✫ ✫ ✫
Quiet: ✫ ✫ ✫ ✫
Security: ✫ ✫ ✫
Cleanliness: ✫ ✫ ✫

Returning toward the entrance station, a left turn into the Heron Harbor Day Use Area will bring you to a protected swimming area and the 5-mile Coyote Run Hiking Trail.

At a little more than an hour from Dallas, this park is a must-visit for anyone needing a weekend escape. After setting up your tent, go explore this 2,560-acre park surrounding a water reservoir with a wildlife management area. The terrain is rolling and covered with oaks, elms, hackberries, and evergreen eastern red cedars. Hiking and equestrian trails also cross areas of prairie, which are a reminder that this portion of Texas still retains a few patches of the great expanses of grassland that run from Texas to the northern plains.

Returning to the main road, travel to Honey Creek Day Use Area or Heron Harbor Day Use Area for some of Texas's best fishing. When the reservoir was created in 1986 by damming the South Sulphur River, a large number of trees were left as habitat for largemouth and white Bass along with catfish and crappie. If you need some exercise, check out 5-mile Coyote Run Trail. This moderately strenuous hiking trail starts and ends in the Heron Harbor parking lot, which is conveniently located next to the swimming area.

Whether on the trail or in the Oak Grove Camping Area, keep watch for the usual white-tailed deer, armadillos, and raccoons in addition to the occasional bald eagle or wild turkey. There is also Doctor's Creek Unit on the north side of the lake, but the camping is primarily for RVs. The area does have additional hiking and biking trails for exploring this 466-acre unit of Cooper Lake State Park.

RECOMMENDED READING

Voices for the Earth: A Treasury of the Sierra Club Bulletin 1893–1977 edited by Ann Gilliam, 1979.

VOICES FROM THE CAMPFIRE

"Get out among the mountains and trees, friend, they will do more for you than either man or woman could" (Theodore Roosevelt to John Muir upon the death of Muir's wife, Louie Wanda, in August 1905).

KEY INFORMATION

ADDRESS: 1690 FM 3505 Sulphur Springs, TX 75482

OPERATED BY: Texas Parks and Wildlife Department

INFORMATION: (903) 945-5256

RESERVATIONS: (512) 389-8900; www.tpwd.state.tx.us

OPEN: All year

SITES: 14

EACH SITE: Fire ring, picnic table, lantern hook, central water

ASSIGNMENT: Reservations get you in the campground; site choice is first come, first served

REGISTRATION: At headquarters

FACILITIES: Modern restrooms and showers on main road

PARKING: Central parking

FEE: $10; $3 per person entrance fee

ELEVATION: 472 feet

RESTRICTIONS: *Pets:* On leash only
Fires: In fire rings only
Alcohol: Prohibited
Vehicles: 2 per site
Other: Maximum 8 persons per site; guests must leave by 10 p.m.; quiet time 10 p.m.–6 a.m.; bring your own firewood or charcoal; pick up main supplies in Sulphur Springs; gathering firewood prohibited

MAP

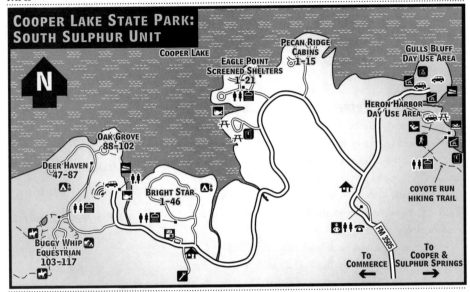

GETTING THERE

From Interstate 30 as it passes through Sulphur Springs, drive north 11.6 miles on Texas 19. Turn left on FM 71 and drive 4.4 miles, then turn right on FM 3505 and drive 1.5 miles to Park Road 8154A.

GPS COORDINATES

UTM Zone (WGS84)   15S
Easting   252494
Northing   3686379
Latitude   N 33.2881°
Longitude   W 95.6578°

DEEP IN THE PINEY WOODS of Northeast Texas, it is easy to imagine the local Caddo Indians traveling along pathways used for centuries to trade with the Choctaw, Cherokee, and the newly arrived European explorers. This popular transportation route was known as the Caddo Trace and was also used for stage routes and mail routes. It was also traveled during the Civil War.

Against this historical backdrop, the Civilian Conservation Corps (CCC) built Daingerfield Sate Park from 1935 to 1938 during the Great Depression, to combat unemployment. The well-worn but durable structures remind us of this difficult period and also leave a legacy of beauty for today's tent campers seeking to get away from the modern economic stresses.

After leaving the headquarters, a left turn at 0.2 miles sends you into rugged wilderness terrain and toward Dogwood Camping Area. These large sites are well spaced with water and electricity. Look for site 17 lakeside on the 80-acre Lake Daingerfield, a no-wake lake for canoes, kayaks, and paddle boats. The area is also known for its dogwoods, cinnamon ferns, and pine-covered hills, where the endangered red-cockaded woodpecker has been known to nest along with its cousin, the large pileated woodpecker. Just listen on a quiet day; you can hear these two beautiful birds hammering for their meal.

Returning on the main road, turn right just before the day-use area toward Cedar Ridge Camping Loop. Turn right at 0.4 miles to this elevated campground and more-primitive sites 47 through 52 backing up to heavy woods. The sites are large and allow a little extra privacy as you get farther from the road.

Leaving this area, the restrooms and showers are directly across the road. To the right is Mountain View Camping Area, which has RVs but also a family-

> *The endangered red-cockaded woodpecker has been known to nest in this area.*

RATINGS

Beauty: ✪ ✪ ✪
Privacy: ✪ ✪
Spaciousness: ✪ ✪ ✪
Quiet: ✪ ✪
Security: ✪ ✪ ✪
Cleanliness: ✪ ✪ ✪

ADDRESS: Route 3, Box 286-B Daingerfield, TX 75638

OPERATED BY: Texas Parks and Wildlife Dept.

INFORMATION: (512) 389-8900; www.tpwd.state .tx.us

OPEN: All year

SITES: 52

EACH SITE: Central water, picnic table, lantern hook, some have electricity

ASSIGNMENT: Reservations get you in the campground; site choice is first come, first served

REGISTRATION: At headquarters

FACILITIES: Modern restrooms and showers at Cedar Ridge/ Mountain View; restrooms at Dogwood

PARKING: At each site

FEE: $12 (water and electric), $8 (water only); $2 entrance fee

ELEVATION: 590 feet

RESTRICTIONS: *Pets:* On leash only *Fires:* In fire rings and grates only *Alcohol:* Prohibited *Vehicles:* 2 per site *Other:* Maximum 8 persons per site; guests must leave by 10 p.m.; quiet time 10 p.m.– 6 a.m.; bring your own firewood or charcoal; limited supplies at headquarters; pick up main supplies in Daingerfield; gathering firewood prohibited

friendly atmosphere. To the left, you return to the day-use area and beautiful views of Lake Daingerfield, without the roar of jet boats or jet skis to interrupt your visit and enjoyment of this deep Northeast Texas park.

While this park may not be well known outside East Texas, it is very popular, so make your reservations early. The 80-acre lake was formed by an earthen dam, which was built by the CCC at the same time as the stone Boat House where you can rent canoes and kayaks. There is also a swimming platform—a reminder that the local swimming hole for many generations was not a cement structure in somebody's backyard.

Camping at this low-key, low-stress park provides the perfect time to read a good book or just sit under a shade tree and reflect upon where modern civilization has taken us and what it has taken away from us. With echoes of the CCC workers building these sturdy structures during the Great Depression, our own economic woes may have the bright side of bringing families and friends back together for the simple pleasures of conversation and face-to-face interaction. Whatever your motivation or purpose, Daingerfield State Park is a good place to start that new life.

RECOMMENDED READING

Ansel Adams: An Autobiography, 1985.

VOICES FROM THE CAMPFIRE

"The fear of death follows from a fear of life. A man who lives fully is prepared to die at any time. . . . Love implies anger. The man who is angered by nothing cares about nothing" (Edward Abbey, *A Voice Crying in the Wilderness*, 1989).

MAP

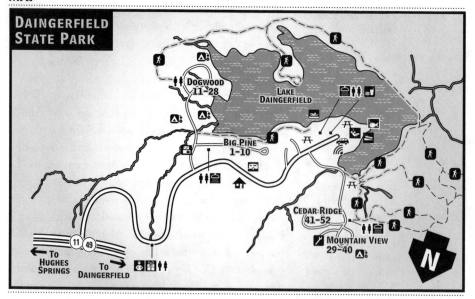

Dogwood
11-28

Lake
Daingerfield

Big Pine
1-10

To
Hughes
Springs

To
Daingerfield

Cedar-Ridge
41-52

Mountain View
29-40

GETTING THERE

From Daingerfield, travel 3
miles east on TX 49. Park
Road 17 is on the left.

GPS COORDINATES

UTM Zone (WGS84)	15S
Easting	342037
Northing	3653943
Latitude	N 33.0125°
Longitude	W 94.6911°

49
LAKE FANNIN
WILDERNESS PARK

> *These primitive sites offer solitude and privacy with a little bit of adventure.*

WHEN LOOKING AT THE TEXAS MAP, the Caddo National Grasslands is a patchwork of heavily treed parkland. In the northwest corner is Lake Fannin and a rediscovered area that it seems time almost forgot. As you travel the gravel road and pass the small sign for Lake Fannin Historical Site, you cross an earthen dam with the scenic and placid lake to the left. Traveling straight ahead, the Lake Fannin Lodge appears on the right, and the 1940s come alive on the wood-plank dance floor, the huge beams overhead, and the three large fireplaces built to heat, not just look good. This rustic and sturdy building was completed in 1938 by the Federal Rural Resettlement Administration as part of the Lake Fannin Organizational Camp. It became a popular destination for both locals and travelers seeking escape from the stress of the Depression, World War II, and the Korean War. It remained open until 1955, when a long period of neglect began that resulted in the lodge, 16 lake cabins, and bathhouse being nearly lost to the ravages of time, weather, and encroaching forest.

But the rebirth has begun, with a group of dedicated volunteers and the U.S. Forest Service combining efforts to restore the park's glory and role as a wilderness getaway from today's stress of war and economic uncertainty.

As you leave the lodge, the campground entrance is on your immediate right and a gravel road leads you into the woods. There are signs for the various campsites, which are still being "found" and cleared for tent use. These primitive sites offer solitude and privacy with a little bit of adventure. Wildlife, including poisonous copperhead snakes, have been found wandering the woods asking who allowed these two-legged invaders into their sanctuary. However, the beauty of the wilderness far outweighs any chance encounter with a

RATINGS

Beauty: ☆ ☆ ☆
Privacy: ☆ ☆ ☆
Spaciousness: ☆ ☆ ☆
Quiet: ☆ ☆ ☆ ☆
Security: ☆ ☆ ☆
Cleanliness: ☆ ☆ ☆

serpent. Just watch where you step or reach and you will avoid any unpleasant encounters.

At present 24 sites have been cleared. The center area has several large sites, which include the old rock fireplaces that still function. These main sites are fairly level, and a sense of history is all around. In this remote location, it's easy to imagine car campers in their 1930s and 40s vehicles pitching a canvas tent for days or even weeks to save money or just enjoy a short vacation from the real world of war and economic turmoil.

If you have a high-clearance vehicle and want more privacy, the other sites are located to the left and right off rock-and-dirt side roads. These sites are on a hillside, so you may have to look for the most level tent spots, but your reward of solitude will be worth it.

As you return to the lodge parking area, a right turn will take you past the caretaker's house and down to the lake's edge, where five of the rustic cabins have been restored for rental and the bathhouse is almost complete. There is also a new 4-mile mountain bike trail and easy launch sites for your canoe or kayak.

As you leave this historical oasis, be sure to stop in Bonham to visit the Sam Rayburn Museum. It honors one of Texas's most powerful political leaders and an early patron of Lake Fannin.

RECOMMENDED READING

Postcards from Ed: Dispatches and Salvos from an American Iconoclast edited by David Peterson, 2006. (Foreword by Terry Tempest Williams.)

VOICES FROM THE CAMPFIRE

"I suppose each of us has his own fantasy of how he wants to die. I would like to go out in a blaze of glory, myself, or maybe simply disappear someday, far out in the heart of the wilderness I love, all by myself, alone with the Universe and whatever God may happen to be looking on. Disappear—and never return" (Edward Abbey in a letter to his father, Paul Revere Abbey, March 14, 1975).

KEY INFORMATION

ADDRESS:	P. O. Box 123 Ivanhoe, TX 75447
OPERATED BY:	Lake Fannin Volunteers and U.S. Forest Service
INFORMATION:	(940) 627-5475 or (903) 583-8402; www.lakefannin.org, www.fs.fed.us/r8/texas
RESERVATIONS:	None
OPEN:	All year
SITES:	Approximately 24
EACH SITE:	Picnic table, rock fireplace
ASSIGNMENT:	First come, first served
REGISTRATION:	At lodge or caretaker's house
FACILITIES:	Modern restrooms at lodge; bathhouse under renovation; pit toilets off campground road
PARKING:	At each site
FEE:	$10 per tent per night
ELEVATION:	598 feet
RESTRICTIONS:	*Pets:* On leash only *Fires:* In fireplaces only *Alcohol:* Prohibited *Vehicles:* 2 per site *Other:* Maximum 8 persons per site; guests must leave by 10 p.m.; quiet time 10 p.m.–6 a.m.; bring your own firewood or charcoal; pick up main supplies in Bonham; gathering firewood prohibited unless down and dead

MAP

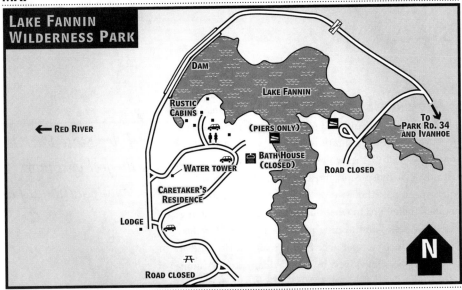

Lake Fannin Wilderness Park — Red River, Dam, Lake Fannin, Rustic Cabins, Water Tower, Caretaker's Residence, Lodge, Bath House (Closed), Piers Only, Road Closed, To Park Rd. 34 and Ivanhoe, N

GETTING THERE

From Bonham, take TX 78 North to FM 1396. Turn right and drive 2.2 miles. Turn left on FM 273 and drive 6 miles. Turn left on Park Road 34 or FM 2035 (a better route). The park entrance is straight ahead.

GPS COORDINATES

UTM Zone (WGS84)   14S
Easting   762866
Northing   3740953
Latitude   N 33.7761°
Longitude   W 96.1614°

A **T ONE TIME OR ANOTHER,** most Texans have traveled on Interstate 20 heading for the eastern United States and those family "vacations" to see relatives or find the white sands (and mosquitos) of Florida. On those trips, most travelers have cruised at high speed past the sign for Tyler State Park with only a quick thought as to what that park might hold. Taking the FM 14 exit and turning north for a mere 2.0 miles, the lucky tent camper will find a real surprise and a 980-acre park developed by the Civilian Conservation Corps between 1935 and 1941. These unemployed men between the ages of 17 and 25 were unwilling victims of the Great Depression and qualified for public assistance. They were paid $30 per month, of which $25 was sent home to their families. In return for back-breaking manual labor, the men received food, clothing, medical care, and a tent over their head. The state of Texas and the nation received beautiful and sturdy structures that form the foundations of many of our most beloved parks, including Tyler State Park.

As you pass the entrance station, note the Whispering Pines Nature Trail on your left, where a quiet walk will lead to many of the plants native to East Texas, including post oaks, blackjack oaks, flowering dogwoods, and redbuds. Be alert to occasional poison ivy and as with all hikes, stay on the marked trail. While enjoying the flora, also watch for the striking red color of the male cardinal, the tufted titmouse, red-bellied woodpeckers, and the ever-present gray squirrels.

Returning to the trailhead, travel 0.4 miles to the Park Road 16 turnoff on your left. This narrow, paved roadway almost immediately plunges you deeper into the forest. The hilly ravine-crossed area has the look and feel of a more-remote national park such as Shenandoah or the Smoky Mountains. The dense understory is sheltered by a 75- to 100-year-old pine-hardwood forest

> *Tyler State Park has the feel of a more remote national park.*

RATINGS

Beauty: ✪ ✪ ✪ ✪
Privacy: ✪ ✪ ✪
Spaciousness: ✪ ✪ ✪
Quiet: ✪ ✪ ✪
Security: ✪ ✪ ✪ ✪
Cleanliness: ✪ ✪ ✪ ✪

ADDRESS: 789 Park Road 16
Tyler, TX 75706

OPERATED BY: Texas Parks
and Wildlife
Department

INFORMATION: (903)597-5338

RESERVATIONS: (512)389-8900;
www.tpwd.state
.tx.us

OPEN: All year

SITES: 39 tent-only sites

EACH SITE: Picnic table, fire
ring, upright char-
coal grate, water

ASSIGNMENT: Reservations get
you in the camp-
ground; site
choice is first
come, first served

REGISTRATION: At headquarters

FACILITIES: Centrally located
showers and mod-
ern restrooms

PARKING: At each site

FEE: $12 water-only
sites; $3 per per-
son entrance fee
ages 13 and older

ELEVATION: 618 feet

RESTRICTIONS: *Pets:* On leash only
Fires: In fire rings
or upright char-
coal grates only
Alcohol: Prohibited
Vehicles: 2 per site
Other: Maximum 8
persons per site;
guests must leave
by 10 p.m.; quiet
time 10 p.m.–
6 a.m.; bring your
own firewood or
charcoal; limited
supplies at park
store; pick up
main supplies in
Tyler; gathering
firewood
prohibited

that acts as a time capsule of what the early pioneers to Texas would have faced as they left their worn-out lands in the east and traveled by foot, horseback, and wagon to the frontier territory of Tejas in search of new farmland or even a new life.

Go past Areas 9 and 10 (shelters) and look for Area 8/Sumac Bend campground 0.6 miles on your right. The campground road leads to sites 142 through 149, which run along a small, seasonal stream and are nicely spaced for privacy. Sites 146 and 149 have the feel of being deep in the woods, and the tall trees are dense enough to provide cool shade even on a hot summer visit.

Returning to the main park road, a right turn after 0.1 miles leads the tent camper to Hickory Hollow and sites 131 through 141. Sites 131, 132, and 134 back up to the same seasonal stream as Sumac Bend, and the sound of birds singing and squirrels racing around fill the otherwise quiet forest. Continue to sites 135 through 138, which border the backwater areas and are large enough for big families to spread out and enjoy the nature trail that crosses the water on a wooden bridge within a few steps of your tent site. Back on the surprisingly hilly main road, a right turn brings you to Area 6/Red Oak campground and sites 117 through 130. These sites are spread on an elevated ridgeline and will get a little more breeze than the lower sites. Sites 124 and 126 have a partial lake view. Sites 118 and 119 are more remote and overlook a dense green canyon (OK, just a really nice ravine). Back at the turnoff, you will find the newly constructed showers and modern restrooms on your immediate left.

Continue on for 0.2 miles to find Area 5/Dogwood Ridge Camping Area and sites 108 through 116. These sites are also elevated, and 111 through 114 have a lake view through the trees.

After leaving Area 5, the remainder of the park drive will take you to the 16 miles of bicycle trails starting at Area 4/Black Jack. Go past RV Area 3/Big Pines (no tents allowed . . . thank goodness) and finish with the lakeside sites of Area 2. While these sites must be shared with the RV crowd, the spacing is adequate and lakefront property does have its advantages.

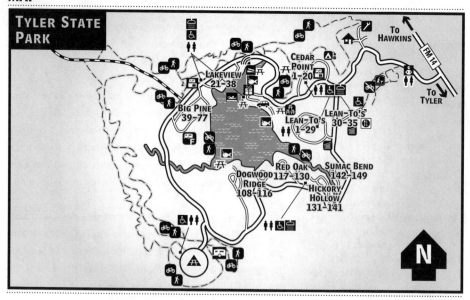

After leaving Area 2, the bathhouse, swimming area, and Browns Point day-use area are 0.5 miles down the road. This area is very inviting on a hot day—be sure to spend a few hours swimming, fishing, or paddling the 64-acre clear spring-fed lake. Whatever activity you choose, this hidden East Texas park is a gem of a forest getaway.

RECOMMENDED READING

An Inconvenient Truth: The Planetary Emergency of Global Warming and What We Can Do About It by Al Gore, 2006.

GPS COORDINATES

UTM Zone (WGS84)	15S
Easting	285414
Northing	3596194
Latitude	N 32.4823°
Longitude	W 95.2836°

VOICES FROM THE CAMPFIRE

"Each person has a sacred duty to use their talents to make a difference. To do otherwise is to waste the very limited time on this earth. To leave a positive legacy is a goal worth pursuing. To inspire others to leave a positive legacy is a gift to the future" (Journal entry of Wendel A. Withrow, October 16, 2004).

APPENDIX A: SOURCES OF INFORMATION

BOOKS AND MAPS

Awbrey, Betty Dooley and Claude Dooley. *Why Stop? A Guide to Texas Historical Roadside Markers,* 5th Edition. 2005.

Big Bend Official National Park Handbook. U.S. Department of the Interior, Washington, D.C.

Gunter, Pete A.Y. *The Big Thicket: An Ecological Reevaluation.* 1993.

Holt, Harold R. *A Birder's Guide to the Texas Coast.* 1993.

Little, Mickey. *Hiking and Backpacking Trails of Texas,* 6th Edition. 2005

MAPSCO. *The Roads of Texas.* 2008

Maxwell, Ross A. *The Big Bend of the Rio Grande: A Guide to the Rocks, Landscape, Geologic History, and Settlers of the Area of Big Bend National Park.* 2008.

Parent, Laurence. *Hiking Big Bend National Park: A Guide to Big Bend's Greatest Hiking Adventures,* 2nd Edition. 2005.

Parent, Laurence. *Official Guide to Texas State Parks and Historic Sites.* 2008.

Peacock, Howard. *Nature Lover's Guide to the Big Thicket.* 1994.

Steely, James Wright and Joseph R. Monticone. *The Civilian Conservation Corps in Texas State Parks.* 1986.

Texas Department of Transportation. *Texas Public Campgrounds: A guide to federal, state and local government administered facilities.* 2006.
Available as a pdf at **www.txdot.gov**

Texas Parks and Wildlife. Texas State Park Guide.
Available as a pdf at **www.tpwd.state.tx.us/publications/parkguide/download**

APPENDIX A: SOURCES OF INFORMATION
[continued]

CONTACT INFORMATION

National Recreation Reservation Service
www.recreation.gov
(877) 444-6777

Texas Department of Transportation: Travel Division
www.traveltex.com
www.txdot.gov
(800) 452-9292

Texas Parks and Wildlife Department
4200 Smith School Road
Austin, TX 78744
www.tpwd.state.tx.us/reserve
(512) 389-8900

U.S. Army Corps of Engineers
www.Corpslakes.us

U.S. Forest Service
www.fs.fed.us

APPENDIX B: CAMPING EQUIPMENT CHECKLIST

COOKING UTENSILS

Aluminum foil

Bottle opener

Can opener

Corkscrew

Cups, plastic or tin

Dish soap (biodegradable), sponge, and towel

Flatware

Frying pan

Fuel for stove

Matches in waterproof container

Plates

Pocketknife

Pot with lid

Salt, pepper, spices, sugar, cooking oil, and maple syrup in spillproof containers

Spatula

Stove

Wooden spoon

FIRST-AID KIT

Antibiotic cream

Band-Aids®

Diphenhydramine (Benadryl®)

Gauze pads

Ibuprofen or aspirin

Insect repellent

Lip balm

Moleskin®

Snakebite kit

Sunscreen

Tape, waterproof adhesive

SLEEPING GEAR

Pillow

Sleeping bag

Sleeping pad, inflatable or insulated

Tent with ground tarp and rainfly

MISCELLANEOUS

Bath soap (biodegradable), washcloth, and towel

Camp chair

Candles

Cooler

Deck of cards

Duct tape

Fire starter

Flashlight or headlamp with fresh batteries

Foul-weather clothing

Paper towels

Plastic zip-top bags

Sunglasses

Toilet paper

Water bottle

Wool or fleece blanket

OPTIONAL

Barbecue grill

Binoculars

Field guides

Fishing rod and tackle

Hatchet

Kayak and related paddling gear

Lantern

Maps (road, topographic, trails, and so on)

Mountain bike and related riding gear

APPENDIX C:
TOP TEN EQUIPMENT
TIPS (FROM SPARTAN
TO LUXURY)

1. Buy a tent big enough to not leave you claustrophobic if weather keeps you inside for a few hours but that doesn't look like a three-bedroom house (unless you brought the entire family for a week's stay).

2. Bring comfortable camp chairs for sitting around the fire.

3. Bring head lamps for those tasks that require both hands free; a small electric lamp for inside your tent (don't forget your journal or a book); and a larger lamp for lighting your cooking area or to set up your tent (turn it off as soon as your fire gets going).

4. Pack a lightweight long-sleeve shirt and pants for cool evenings or early mornings.

5. Spend the extra money to get two premium ground pads and extra-wide sleeping bags. Remember, you're not backpacking, so weight and size are not a concern.

6. Bring proper-fitting hiking boots, water bottles, hats, and sun protection.

7. Bring your own dry firewood and kindling. Avoid newspaper as a starter material. A small amount of solid fireplace starter or self-lighting charcoal will help in bad weather. Pack your stove on every trip in case of a burn ban or specific cooking need.

8. Slip-on camp shoes with rubber soles are a must after a long day of hiking or for walks to the bathroom. Water shoes or sandals will serve this purpose unless weather dictates otherwise.

9. Cookware should be non-stick to assist in clean-up. If you have a perfectly seasoned cast-iron skillet or dutch oven, be sure you bring the necessary tools to clean it.

10. Food selection can be the highlight of any tent-camping experience. Fill the ice chest with goodies, but remember that this is supposed to be a vaction for everyone, including the cook and clean-up crew.

INDEX

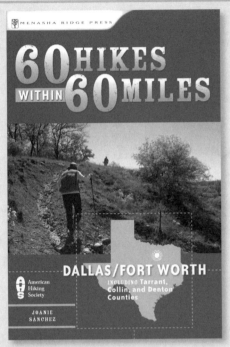

60 Hikes within 60 Miles: Houston

by Laurie Roddy
ISBN: 978-0-89732-958-3
301 pages 6x9, paperback, $16.95
maps, photographs, inde

Houston's wealth of hiking trails is astounding! Hikes explore old native homesteads, native prairies, deep forests, riparian woodlands, urban byways, wildlife preserves along the Great Texas Coastal Birding Trail, wetlands, and the 138-mile-long Lone Star Trail.

With our "Key-At-A-Glance" info for each hike you'll have a quick assessment of the trail before you go on your hike.

Laurie Roddy has done all the advance scouting for you, all that's left to do is enjoy the hike!

60 Hikes within 60 Miles:
San Antonio and Austin

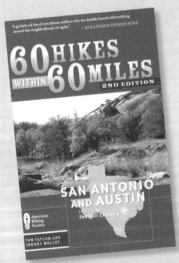

by Tom Taylor and Johnny Molloy
ISBN: 978-0-89732-725-1
226 pages, 6x9, paperback
2nd edition $16.95
maps, photographs, index

Local author Tom Taylor and coauthor Johnny Molloy introduce newcomers as well as lifelong residents to a surprising array of the best day hikes within an hour's drive of San Antonio and Austin. Filled with detail, this guide leaves no stone unturned in the quest for the best hiking in the area.

With all the advance scouting done for you, all you need to do is enjoy the breathtaking beauty in and around San Antonio and Austin.

MENASHA RIDGE PRESS
www.menasharidge.com

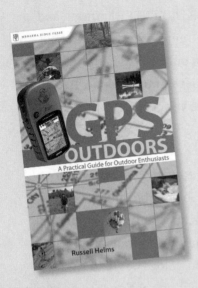

DEAR CUSTOMERS AND FRIENDS,

SUPPORTING YOUR INTEREST IN OUTDOOR ADVENTURE, travel, and an active lifestyle is central to our operations, from the authors we choose to the locations we detail to the way we design our books. Menasha Ridge Press was incorporated in 1982 by a group of veteran outdoorsmen and professional outfitters. For 25 years now, we've specialized in creating books that benefit the outdoors enthusiast.

Almost immediately, Menasha Ridge Press earned a reputation for revolutionizing outdoors- and travel-guidebook publishing. For such activities as canoeing, kayaking, hiking, backpacking, and mountain biking, we established new standards of quality that transformed the whole genre, resulting in outdoor-recreation guides of great sophistication and solid content. Menasha Ridge continues to be outdoor publishing's greatest innovator.

The folks at Menasha Ridge Press are as at home on a white-water river or mountain trail as they are editing a manuscript. The books we build for you are the best they can be, because we're responding to your needs. Plus, we use and depend on them ourselves.

We look forward to seeing you on the river or the trail. If you'd like to contact us directly, join in at www.trekalong.com or visit us at www.menasharidge.com. We thank you for your interest in our books and the natural world around us all.

SAFE TRAVELS,

Bob Sehlinger

BOB SEHLINGER
PUBLISHER